T0269960

THE JOURNEY OF LEADERSHIP

THE JOURNEY OF LEADERSHIP

LEADERSHIP

*How CEOs Learn to Lead
from the Inside Out*

**DANA MAOR, HANS-WERNER KAAS,
KURT STROVINK, and RAMESH SRINIVASAN**

Senior Partners, McKinsey & Company

PORTFOLIO | PENGUIN

Portfolio / Penguin
An imprint of Penguin Random House LLC
penguinrandomhouse.com

Most Portfolio books are available at a discount when purchased in quantity for sales
promotions or corporate use. Special editions, which include personalized covers, excerpts,
and corporate imprints, can be created when purchased in large quantities. For more
information, please call (212) 572-2232 or e-mail specialmarkets@penguinrandomhouse
.com. Your local bookstore can also assist with discounted bulk purchases using the Penguin
Random House corporate Business-to-Business program. For assistance in locating a
participating retailer, e-mail B2B@penguinrandomhouse.com.

Library of Congress Cataloging-in-Publication Data
Names: Maor, Dana, author. | Kaas, Hans-Werner, author. |
Strovink, Kurt, author. | Srinivasan, Ramesh, author.
Title: The journey of leadership: how CEOs learn to lead from the inside out /
Dana Maor, Hans-Werner Kaas, Kurt Strovink, and Ramesh Srinivasan.
Description: First edition. | New York: Portfolio, [2024] |
Includes bibliographical references and index.
Identifiers: LCCN 2024007432 (print) | LCCN 2024007433 (ebook) |
ISBN 9780593714218 (hardcover) | ISBN 9780593714225 (ebook)
Subjects: LCSH: Leadership. | Executive ability. | Success in business.
Classification: LCC HD57.7 .M39156 2024 (print) |
LCC HD57.7 (ebook) | DDC 303.3/4—dc23/eng/20240222
LC record available at https://lccn.loc.gov/2024007432
LC ebook record available at https://lccn.loc.gov/2024007433

Printed in the United States of America
1st Printing

BOOK DESIGN BY NICOLE LAROCHE

While the author has made every effort to provide accurate telephone numbers,
internet addresses, and other contact information at the time of publication,
neither the publisher nor the author assumes any responsibility for errors or for changes
that occur after publication. Further, the publisher does not have any control over and
does not assume any responsibility for author or third-party websites or their content.

CONTENTS

Part 2

MOVING BEYOND YOURSELF

INTRODUCTION

O n yet another perfect day in Northern California, a group of CEOs from various industries filed into an airy conference room with tall windows overlooking lush hills. Wine country's renowned weather and scenic views weren't the main attraction, however; these leaders came here to pause, reflect, learn, and develop, which is hard to do when you're busy at work. What they talk about will surprise you. At this session—one of McKinsey & Company's Bower Forum programs for CEO leadership development—the conversation, as always, started with strategy, operations, finances, talent, and other topics you'd expect executives to care about, but soon enough, we started to explore issues that can be hard to share anywhere but there.

A CEO of a major biotech company started talking about how he was struggling to lead his company into the future. He had a very powerful board whose members had their own strong opinions about the direction of the firm. He complained that every time he tried to initiate a bold move, his directors tried to push him in a different direction. He felt tentative and frustrated.

The other CEOs in the room started to ask him about his skills, his knowledge, and his vision for the company. Ramesh, one of the authors of this book and a Bower Forum coach, encouraged the CEO to think about why he felt insecure given his talent and his in-depth knowledge of the industry. "I asked him," recalls Ramesh, "to think about how much he has actually put into the business and the commitment he has made and that he should focus on what his investors and patients want."

The biotech CEO started to gradually open up to the others. He was learning how to get to know himself better, to recognize his strengths, to set aside his biases, and to understand that he needed to listen more closely to others and deliver on what his constituents wanted. As the retreat came to a close, everyone who had been in the room with the CEO saw a changed person, someone with a deeper self-awareness and a renewed sense of confidence—someone willing to make bold moves. It was no coincidence that the executive went on to build one of the most financially and scientifically successful biotech firms in the world.

As McKinsey senior partners, we have worked closely with hundreds of leaders like this biotech CEO, who hail from both Fortune Global 500 corporations and leading nonprofits. Two of us, Hans-Werner and Ramesh, are co-deans of McKinsey's Bower Forum CEO leadership development program, a two-day event where over the last ten years more than 500 of the world's top CEOs and business leaders—in aggregate they oversee 13 million employees—have opened their hearts and minds to confront personal and professional challenges. One of our co-authors, Dana, is the global co-head and European leader of McKinsey's People & Organizational Performance Practice. She partners with organizations to build leaders and talent and also coaches at the Bower Forum. Our other coauthor, Kurt, leads McKinsey's global CEO Initiative to help build great CEOs and CEO counselors. The Bower program is the culmination of the best thinking on leadership at McKinsey, whose roughly 3,000 partners work with 7,000 corporate clients around the world. Here McKinsey's best practices in leadership are put to work, offering CEOs a proven approach to reinvent themselves. We want to share with you what the four of us have learned from coaching some of the world's best leaders, both from working with them at the Bower Forum and through our consulting practices at McKinsey.

Over the years, we've seen that the best leaders learn to become more self-aware and self-reflective. They realize that the brake that's holding them back as they're trying to press the accelerator is their own psychological conditioning, which is rooted in the habits and behaviors that, ironically, got them where they are. We offer in this book a step-by-step approach for leaders to reinvent themselves both professionally and personally. It is a journey that helps a person change the psychological, emotional, and ultimately the human attributes of leadership that can prevent them from reaching the highest levels of excellence.

We first became interested in the human side of leadership after seeing many skilled people who had mastered all the right executive skills—financial acumen, strategic and operational management, and system thinking—and who felt confident and powerful yet struggled to link their vision for success with the actual performance of their organizations and failed to spark passion in their employees. They would lead their team with a rousing battle cry, only to turn and see that no one was following them or, at best, that employees were following them without enthusiasm and energy.

After a careful analysis of what was holding back these otherwise talented leaders, we concluded that on a deep, psychological level they were not authentically connecting with themselves and, equally important, with others on their team. At the Bower Forum programs and other McKinsey leadership development sessions we led, everyone knew how to define and acquire the logical, tangible skills of leadership. But when we asked how they could become both a logical and a human-centric leader—one who is more self-aware, empathetic, humble, reflective, vulnerable, and consequently more inspiring, resilient, and balanced—the pathway to acquiring those personal attributes was much harder to describe. A survey of Bower Forum participants found that 57 percent came to the program for personal challenges—including becoming a more human, versatile leader and a stronger leader of teams—a higher percentage than those who came to work on their strategies. (See pages 246–47 for more detailed results from our survey.) Becoming a more human leader is a journey often traveled without much help or guidance. Some of the best said they were simply born with those qualities, while others said they were fortunate to meet some great personal coaches along the way, but no one could point to a clear road map to becoming a more authentic and human-centric leader. That is what this book attempts to do—to describe, explain, and codify a leader's inner journey, in essence leading from the inside out. This is the key ingredient to make a lasting impact as you lead your teams and the broader organization.

This journey is nuanced and complex. It calls for personal growth, which means one has to be constantly learning, listening, inspiring, and caring, gradually reinventing oneself as a leader. Leadership is not only about those seemingly endless things you need to do when you're an amazing CEO but also about being aware of who you are as a person and always improving as a human being. It's all about how you change yourself and others. It's about adopting a human-centric leadership approach.

Most executives don't spend enough time thinking about the personal side of leadership. As Dana recalls, "I spent months working with a CEO on their agenda: strategy, execution, and metrics. Over the course of our journey we also touched on culture, what leadership means, and how that should impact the organization. That was a topic, however, that took up only a small part of our formal program. After a year of working together, as we were reflecting on our work, the CEO said, 'Our partnership made a difference on multiple dimensions. But the one thing that made the biggest difference, the turning point that changed how we operated, was that conversation we had on the sidewalk after dinner a year ago, where you suggested I should think more about culture and how I have to change as a person to inspire this cultural journey in the organization. That was the moment my focus shifted, and I knew what to work on."

When we started our careers at McKinsey, the world was a very different place. Investors, boards, and the business press worshipped the imperial CEO. Larger-than-life leaders such as GE's Jack Welch or Chrysler's Lee Iacocca were household names. These all-knowing, tough-minded, results-oriented individuals made frequent appearances on television talk shows and wrote bestselling business books. Their employees revered them, hung on their every word, and expected them to have all the answers. They and they alone called the plays.

The imperial CEO is done. Yes, leaders such as Elon Musk and Mark Zuckerberg get headlines and have become internet memes, but even they can't go it alone. They have surrounded themselves with superb executives, inventors, and innovators. Today leaders must take up a new mantle. Unlike the authority figures of the past, this new cohort does not pretend to have all the answers. Gone are the days when a leader barks an order or throws out a plan and everyone falls lockstep in line.

The winning formula is for leaders to be aware of all the signals, both verbal and nonverbal, that they are giving, and of the weight they carry—

to stay in touch with their emotions, be sensitive to how they interact with others, and ensure the authenticity of their actions. To add value, they listen, experiment, and learn from others, balancing competing commitments and short- and long-term objectives, keeping in mind the demands of their many stakeholders. They enable their teams and colleagues to succeed and contribute with passion and confidence. The best then learn how to balance these human-centric attributes with the hard-nosed skills that helped them win the top job. This is the new model, and sooner or later everyone worth their management salt encounters a moment when they realize that leadership has as much to do with leading themselves as it does with leading others. At that crucial moment, they switch from the traditional leader they thought they *should* be to one who is adopting a human leadership approach. They start learning and growing to meet the demands of their position and to fulfill their boldest aspirations.

Being a senior leader is a lonely role, and many feel adrift in today's fast-paced and ever-evolving business landscape, which is rife with volatility, complexity, and ambiguity. "The only training for being a CEO is being a CEO," observed Marvin Bower, McKinsey's longest-serving global managing partner, who alongside James O. McKinsey defined and shaped the foundations of the firm in the twentieth century. It's little wonder that a study by Development Dimensions International found that 83 percent of leaders across the world felt they were unprepared for their new leadership roles.

This shift to a more humble and open form of leadership is happening because circumstances demand it. The terrain is shifting rapidly, making the old tried-and-true leadership maps all but useless. Boosting the bottom line is necessary but not sufficient. Today's leaders must master such complex issues as digital transformation, inflation, disrupted global supply chains, scarce talent, a lack of diversity, cybersecurity, and climate change, as well as an awakened search for purpose in employees. This means that no one person, no matter how brilliant or capable, has the experience, knowledge, or temperament to tackle all these challenges alone. Little wonder that the CEO job has gotten more precarious. According to the executive compensation firm Equilar, from 2013 to 2022 the average CEO tenure at S&P 500 companies has decreased 20 percent from six years to just under five years.

There's another reason why human leadership has become so crucial to organizations these days. With the rapid onset of artificial intelligence (AI) and generative AI (GenAI) in the workplace, an increasing number of repetitive and analytical management tasks such as market analysis, project management, budgets, customer service, decision making, and fact finding will be handled by AI algorithms, assuming the software keeps improving. If you are a traditional leader who's great at numbers, planning, and scheduling, your job might be threatened. Going forward, the differentiating factor will be human leadership that gives people a sense of purpose and inspires them, and that cares about who they are and what they're thinking and feeling. Many employees today believe that much of the technical and analytical guidance they need is more easily obtained from AI solutions. A survey conducted by the research firm Potential Project found that employees already have more confidence in AI than in their human bosses in certain areas of leadership and in the management of certain tasks. Why not, if they can get the job done without feeling neglected or abused by their manager?

Tapping into AI alone, however, will not lead to high performance. What employees really long for in their leaders is development, experience, care, and wisdom. The best companies know that leadership—to put it pointedly—is about more than management; it is also about embracing the human element. They will combine the analytical advantages of AI with leaders who have excellent people skills to drive their organizations to new heights. AI can offer a twofold benefit. By supporting or replacing analytical and technical tasks, it can free up more time for leaders to spend on human leadership. Second, AI can provide analytical and results-oriented insights on the effectiveness of human-centric leadership, giving leaders constant feedback on the effectiveness of their human leadership style, on how they're leading from the inside out.

A leadership approach that balances financial performance, AI/Gen-AI, and people can not only help CEOs succeed in their jobs but can also pay dividends. That's because when human capital is managed the right way, the results translate straight to the bottom line. According to a 2023 McKinsey Global Institute study of eighteen hundred large companies across all sectors in fifteen countries, those businesses that focused on human capital development *in addition to* financial performance were roughly one and a half times more likely to remain high performers over time and have about half the earnings volatility. In fact, when the COVID-19 pandemic hit, they maintained profitability and grew revenues twice as fast as companies that focused mainly on financial performance.

In this book we explore how CEOs should lead themselves and then lead others through personal and organizational change. Learning, growth, and self-reinvention start with introspection, and the CEOs we portray in these pages have embarked on a profound exploration of who they are and what they stand for. Their stories reveal what they learned over the course of their careers, and how they've applied those teachings to real-world situations. Many of these stories come from our Bower

Forum sessions, where typically three to five CEOs from noncompeting companies deeply engage with one another, privately share experiences and aspirations, and challenge one another on topics and offer advice, including how to lead from the inside out. These sessions operate under Chatham Rules, providing CEOs with a safe place where they can drop their public face and work through problems with peers who understand what they're going through. (We obtained permission from attendees whose stories appear in the book and disguised identities in a few cases when necessary.) A few select McKinsey senior partners act as Bower Forum faculty, and two experienced former CEOs cohost each event. (For more detail about how the Bower Forum works, see the appendix on page 248.)

The insights you'll read about in more detail in this book, which have come out of not only the Bower Forum but also from McKinsey's leadership practices, include the following:

- To combat the fact that no one would tell him bad news, the CEO of a media company cultivated "truth tellers" at every level of the organization.
- A CEO mustered the courage to feel that she belonged in a male-dominated industry.
- The head of a pharmaceutical company used a deep learning technique to predict the severity of the COVID-19 pandemic, which gave his company a jump on producing a new vaccine.
- The president of a large foundation overcame impostor syndrome, where she had struggled with doubts about her own abilities.

- To enable better decision making, an admiral who led U.S. special operations forces trained his teams to respond to changes in the terrain rather than to stick to a preconceived plan.
- The head of a major hospital found that the best way to lead is to connect with employees on an emotional level.
- By humbling himself and treating his employees like family, a CEO turned a manufacturing company around and then weathered the 2008 financial crisis without layoffs.
- The CEO of an auto supply company grew it into a global powerhouse by figuring out how to leverage the tricky psychological balance between motivating people and pressuring them to make the numbers.
- The leader of an industrial, aerospace, and defense company learned to become more versatile in order to build the new skills he needed to navigate a fast-changing world.
- Before coaching his top executives, a CEO of a global auto company took the time to learn more about their life stories and personal issues.

We've designed our leadership process to have two main parts—one focused on the psychological, emotional, and human aspect of leading yourself, called "It Starts with You," and one focused on the human side of leading teams and building organizations, called "Moving beyond Yourself." In other words, how do CEOs learn to lead from the inside out?

In the first part of the process, we help you to learn how to listen to your inner self, and how to overcome your own barriers and biases. What is it you really want to accomplish? What assumptions are you making—including about yourself—that stand in the way? This requires that you assess your situation in an unbiased manner. Here we help you learn how to deeply listen to your network of stakeholders who can help you understand their own needs and offer advice to you as a leader. The result is a deeper self-awareness and self-reflection that helps you develop a clear inner compass for navigating competing views and for finding the confidence and resilience to make the right decisions—all while embracing a more human leadership approach.

How CEOs Learn to Lead from the Inside Out: A Human-Centric Leadership Approach

PART 1
Lead from the inside out:
It starts with you

1. Humility
2. Confidence
3. Selflessness
4. Vulnerability
5. Resilience
6. Versatility

PART 2
Lead from the inside out:
Moving beyond yourself

7. Embed purpose
8. Inspire boldness
9. Empower people
10. Encourage truth telling
11. Adopt fearless learning
12. Instill empathy

The Journey of Leadership never ends:
Find your forum for continual reinvention

Part 2 of *The Journey of Leadership* is all about unleashing the potential of your people and making positive change in your organization by leveraging the aspirations, the deeper self-awareness, and the human leadership attributes that you cultivated in part 1. In other words, once leaders know how to lead their inner selves, they are prepared to lead individuals, teams, and systems from the inside out. We explore how to deliver on your mandate in a way that enacts true change in an organization. You learn how to engage your team in your radical plan for change, to get them to speak truth to power, to be flexible when unexpected circumstances hit, to feel a sense of purpose, and to be willing to go the extra mile to make the business a success.

We're not by any means suggesting that leaders abandon their hard-nosed, analytical leadership skills. The challenge is to balance them with their soft leadership skills. Think of it as a professional tennis player who masters all the basic strokes—forehand, backhand, serve—but then must balance that technical knowledge with resilience, psychological toughness, and an understanding of their opponent's strengths and weaknesses. A player who is only technically excellent will rarely win big tournaments.

One of our coauthors and a Bower Forum coach, Hans-Werner Kaas, points out that an executive's ability to balance seemingly contradictory mindsets is a topic that gets a lot of play these days. At one program, the participants were struggling to balance the need for a CEO to be confident about the company's strategy with a desire to encourage their teams to question existing plans and redefine them. As one Bower Forum participant framed it, "Developing such a differentiated culture and capability is essential for my organization." Hans-Werner's co-faculty partner Admiral Eric Olson, the former head of the U.S. Special Operations Command, explained to the group that the best leaders are versatile, taking different approaches based on a current understanding of the situation. A CEO might be heavily invested in a well-defined, rigorous plan, but the best leaders balance that with the understanding that they and their teams must be ready and capable to adjust—or at times completely redefine—plans based on changing external and internal circumstances. As Olson put it to the group and as he has emphasized with the Navy SEALs, "When the map differs from the terrain, then go with the terrain."

INTRODUCTION

Hans-Werner uses this insight to discuss the importance of what we call the five balancing acts of CEOs, a major takeaway for many of the CEOs who attend our Bower Forums.

Great leaders balance:

1. Being certain about what they know *and* discovering new ideas and approaches (including adjusting original plans) through rapid, creative, and unbiased reassessments and learning.
2. An obsession with financial performance with the needs of all the company's shareholders and stakeholders.
3. Being a steward of the business with being someone who occasionally takes bold and well-calculated risks and moves when opportunities arise.
4. Being in control with empowering teams to take the initiative.
5. Being a hardheaded professional with someone who takes a more humane approach.

To succeed, today's leaders must learn to master these polarities. They must be humble yet decisive, vulnerable yet strong, cautious yet bold, forgiving yet demanding, and certain but willing to change. As F. Scott Fitzgerald put it in *The Crack-Up*, "The test of a first-rate intelligence is the ability to hold two opposed ideas in mind at the same time, and still retain the ability to function."

Our ultimate goal is to encourage CEOs and other leaders who radically focus on financial performance to unleash their inner visionary and their leadership potential—to become someone who can see multiple possibilities for personal and organizational growth and generate a holistic impact for all stakeholders. We want to take command-and-control-minded executives and teach them to act as more human leaders and partners who collaborate in empowered networks. We help leaders who rule and control through their own sense of certainty switch to a mindset of rapid, deep learning and discovery. And finally, we hope to persuade them to see the world in all its wonderful diversity and to be their best authentic selves.

If some of the world's best CEOs have discovered the importance of the human side of leadership and have taken the time to go deep within themselves to build that capability, then surely this approach will be valuable to many others in all types of organizations. Our humble hope is that if you apply this inside-out approach for change to yourself, your team, and all your employees, you will be well on your way to becoming a great human-centric leader and an inspiring role model in your organization and beyond.

Part 1

IT STARTS WITH YOU

1

Humility

YOU'RE NOT THE SMARTEST PERSON IN THE ROOM

A t a Bower Forum meeting held in Frankfurt, Germany, the CEO of an Asian tech giant explained how he had an extremely complicated relationship with his board. The chairman had been the previous CEO for twenty years and had helped build the company into a powerhouse. The trouble was that the chairman was still heavily involved in running the company, making it very difficult for the CEO to do his job. The CEO knew he needed to make major changes in the company, but he was struggling to get any agreement from the chairman, who ruled with an iron fist. While the CEO felt shackled, he also was conflicted because the chairman was his mentor and he wanted to stay loyal and figure out a way to work collaboratively with him.

One of the other CEOs in the room said, "You can't do this on your own. First off, to work more collaboratively with your chairman you have to understand him better and figure out who are his influencers on the board and who are his friends. You need to talk to these people and get useful input on what the chairman is thinking and then figure out how to influence him." The first CEO explained to the group that an Indonesian investment fund, which controlled some 30 percent of the company, had a strong relationship with the chairman and influenced his views. The CEO, however, didn't have any sort of relationship with them. The other CEOs at the forum told him he needed to fly to Indonesia and start reporting quarterly results in person to the fund managers. That way he could get to know them and ask for their help in persuading the chairman to work with him to make the changes he needed.

Then another CEO chimed in: "Once you understand what your chairman is thinking, you should have a frank conversation with him where you lay out the facts and arguments for your strategic plan. But don't hit him all at once. Have a series of discussions laying out your agenda in bite-sized chunks and tell him, 'Here's what I'm thinking about at this point in time.' Then tell him you'd like to come back in another week and talk more, and then keep doing that until he's won over."

Over the next several months, the CEO reached within himself, realizing that he indeed couldn't go it alone. He sought out investors, friends of the chairman, and others, asking their advice on what the chairman was thinking and the best ways to approach him. Eventually the two rivals began to see eye-to-eye on the company's strategy and worked together to move the business forward.

The CEO of this Asian tech giant is a great example of a leader who benefited from the first element of the Bower Forum process. He took an unbiased look at himself and realized that he was stalled at his job and didn't have all the answers. He realized he needed to become a better listener and reach out to those who could help him perform better. He then built an outside network of advisers to help him figure out how to work with his chairman to form a mandate for change. He had been trying to go it alone, but after feedback from other CEOs he came to realize that he is not expected to go it alone. He wasn't always the smartest one in the room.

As this CEO proved, personal change is possible. After much self-assessment, he became more open and humble, seeking input from his management team, outsiders, and the board, who had a broader sense of the business context or knew the thinking of the company's chairman. He learned how to embark on a never-ending learning journey, one where he had the courage to reach out and listen to the advice of others.

One of the key reasons CEOs come to the forum is to address their isolation and their loneliness. No one likes to feel lonely, but when you get the top job, that's just what happens. Sometimes no one talks to you because you act like you're the smartest one in the room, and no one wants to say the wrong thing or bring bad news to the boss. As a *New Yorker* cartoon that showed a CEO addressing his team put it, "I am more than willing to acknowledge my mistakes if someone is stupid enough to point them out to me."

When they are feeling uncertain and lack confidence, many CEOs tend to go "one up"—convincing themselves that they are more important in order to feel safer in their role. (Later in the book we will explore how the best leaders go "one down" and behave in ways that supercharge teamwork.) Going one up is a move into grandiosity that leads them to think that they are better and smarter than everyone else. The leaders who fall into this trap aren't usually conceited people, but they might believe the job requires that they make decisions on their own—something that in reality isn't required. As former Warren Buffett sidekick and legendary investor Charlie Munger once put it, "Smart, hard-working people aren't exempted from professional disasters from overconfidence. Often, they just go aground in the more difficult voyages they choose, relying on their self-appraisals that they have superior talents and methods."

Sometimes going one up is a personal attribute of the CEO—they intrinsically operate that way to overcome their own insecurities. Other times, it is the team that expects the CEO to be decisive and have all the answers. This can create disempowerment or even fear in the organization. Teams will defer to the CEO and wait for them to come up with the answer. When tough problems arose at meetings, one CEO of a media company would become very verbose, take over, and solve the problem on the table. This kind of behavior can be very intimidating. What makes this pattern difficult to catch is that it was often rewarded in the past, and it feels good—the CEO gets a rush of energy.

Acting like you're above it all can have dire consequences, as history shows. Napoleon Bonaparte was a brilliant military strategist and conqueror, but he also believed that he was smarter than everyone else and was often unwilling to listen to the advice of his advisers. Ignoring the warnings of his generals, he decided in 1812 that his path to victory in Europe included an invasion of Russia. A fierce winter and tough resistance shattered his forces. Napoleon's army entered Russia with more than 612,000 men, and only 112,000 remained after the campaign. His reputation of invincibility was shattered.

Believing that your colleagues expect you to have all the answers is a trap—one that can have dire consequences in the business world. In the 1970s, former GM executive John DeLorean founded the DeLorean Motor Company, which made a futuristic stainless-steel-bodied sports car with gull-wing doors. He was known for his charisma and innovative ideas but also had a reputation for being arrogant and unwilling to listen to others. While others cautioned him to move slowly—starting a car company is a highly complex endeavor—he ultimately overextended the company's finances, and the production of the DeLorean sports car became a financial disaster that led to the company's bankruptcy.

With this in mind, leaders attending the Bower Forum try to honestly define their attributes—do they always think they have the answer, do they interrupt their colleagues before they have the opportunity to finish their thought, are they the type of person who already knows the answer before they walk into the room? We then suggest that they work on skills that will help them unlearn this unproductive behavior. We suggest they ask themselves what is the worst that would happen if they stopped acting like they're the smartest one in the room and opened themselves up to the opinions and thoughts of others. If they *really* listened? Even if what they hear contradicts the way they see the world, what do you have to lose? In today's fast-changing landscape, it's less about what an individual knows and more about knowing what they need to know and where to get it. This means developing the skills to really hear what others have to say instead of looking for validation of what you already think.

The best leaders realize they don't have all the answers and regularly question and listen to those around them. Listening sounds easy, yet it is one of the most challenging skills for senior leaders who have been rewarded through their career for their decisiveness, their ability to be in control, and their confidence. Most who make it to the CEO level are, of course, super smart, but their true value comes from their unique bird's-eye view, their ability to connect the dots and bring multiple perspectives together. And to do that well, they have to apply their experience and wisdom in a different way. Instead of going one up, they think carefully about what they hear, they reflect, and they actively understand root causes and implications. They create circles of advisers who can help guide them, give them opposing views, and encourage them to adopt new perspectives. They make it a habit to go beyond their comfort zone, to engage in fearless learning, ready to question deeply anchored assumptions and beliefs. In short, they know that they're not the smartest person in the room.

That raises the question: Who do you need to listen to? It depends on which problems you're trying to solve. Generally speaking, if it's an operation or process you're trying to improve, you listen to what your direct reports and sometimes those managers two or three levels below you have to say. For strategic direction or big personnel decisions, generally speaking, it's the board and your most trusted investors, but if the change is big enough, customer and clients should be included. For products and services, it's the customer, of course. For societal issues and the company's purpose, it never hurts to get input from your employees and the communities where you operate. In all cases you need to listen for different perspectives, while trying to understand the underlying motivations both by what the speaker says and also through nuances such as their tone and body language.

Most important, by opening themselves up to new ideas, leaders can build a mandate—which means persuading the board, investors, and other constituents to grant you the authority to carry out your strategy. As a CEO, nobody tells you exactly what you should do, so it's your job to figure out your mandate. In this age of stakeholder capitalism, you have to establish a mandate with your customers, with your employees, with your investors, with society at large, and with your family. You need to be open enough to listen to what they have to say without any biases or preconceived notions. It's helpful to have what we call an inside-out mindset. You need to find the right balance between understanding the company as an insider and reflecting on it as an outsider—as if you're an outsider coming in to understand your company's culture, context, and legacy.

The best leaders take the time early in their tenure to ask "What is my mandate?" and get input from a broad set of stakeholders—even if they're an insider who's been with the company for years and think they know what needs to be done. It's also very important to understand that mandates evolve over time. Early in a CEO tenure there might be one or two critical things that need immediate attention, which if you ignore could result in a crisis. Later on, once you've settled in your role, you have an opportunity to establish an even bolder, broader mandate to drive change, whether it be your own company or the broader system.

Reflecting on that mandate and then thinking about the unique challenges that come in the way of accomplishing it can be quite helpful for CEOs. Through listening and a willingness to change their minds, they win permission from their various constituents to act. Without a mandate, many well-meaning leaders attempt to forge ahead yet fail, dragged down by the weight of a reluctant organization or the intransigence of board members and investors who aren't aligned with their vision.

We are, of course, not suggesting that you hand over your power to those working for you. Quite the contrary. Excellent leaders run a participatory process where they listen to different points of view, but the final decision still rests with the CEO. "Your point of view could change," says Mark Fields, the former CEO of Ford Motor and a Bower coach, "but it can't be, 'Hey, let's just figure this out together, and everybody's going to have a vote.'" This is one of the polarities that leaders need to master. They have to be humble but at the same time have the wits and strength to make a tough decision—especially when there's little consensus on the team.

Many CEOs have struggled with how to get their management teams aligned and marching in the same direction. It's a tight balancing act. As the CEO, you've got to listen to others and perhaps at times change your mind, but at the end of the day you have to call the shots. And as we'll explore in part 2 of this book, you must pull this off in such a way that your team gets behind the plan because you've appealed to both their heads and their hearts. Appealing to the head is laying out the reality—here's what we think are the opportunities. The heart is linking the plan to the mission of the company. Is this something we're passionate about? What do we want our legacy to be? Do we want it to be one of failure, or do we want it to be one of success?

Getting a team pulling in the same direction is hard to do because, as we'll see in chapter 10, "Everyone Keeps Things from the Boss," even direct reports don't want to tell the CEO what's going on in the company. No one wants to bring bad news. No one wants to irritate the CEO, because they fear it will throw their career back if they're the one who's always saying, "This isn't right," or, "I don't agree with what you're doing."

So the job of the CEO is to learn how to engage in what we call positive leadership, which means listening and trying to elicit ideas from others without reacting negatively to what they're telling you. Says Fields, "I've seen great examples of how a leader reacted in a positive way when bad news came up. They thanked the person for sharing and in the process created a safe place for others to bring up criticism. I've also seen absolutely godawful examples where a person gives bad news, and the leader just eviscerates them. That teaches everybody else in that room to keep their mouth shut."

Another advantage of listening closely is that it not only makes people feel good, but it also helps you understand how people on your team come to decisions. You can evaluate their thought processes every day, how they're thinking and whether they're growing in the job. "If the person comes up with the wrong ideas too often," says Fields, "you might say, 'I can't be patient with this person anymore. Maybe they don't belong here.'"

Says another Bower coach, "The leaders who get into trouble are those who think that they have all the answers, who don't listen well, and who are arrogant, narcissistic, grandiose, only interested in money and not caring enough about the business and the people."

Humility and openness also come into play when you are struggling to make a big, game-changing decision. To make sure they're on the right track, the best CEOs reach out and have candid conversations with their different stakeholders. They have the humility to listen carefully to their advice and the willingness to act on it. These leaders see depending on others not as a weakness but as a crucial tool to arrive at the right solution.

Throughout his long career, Dan Vasella, the former CEO of pharmaceutical giant Novartis and a coach at the Bower Forum, says that a big reason for his success was his ability to listen to others to form the best plan to execute his mandate. Often he found himself reaching out to others for advice. While navigating his company through the fast-changing and consolidating global pharmaceutical industry, he at times felt like he was dragging a boat through wet sand. Vasella, a physician and marketing executive at the Swiss pharma company Sandoz, was named CEO of the firm in 1992. He knew Sandoz wasn't big or powerful enough to keep thriving in this rapidly evolving industry. He needed to ease his company's reliance on the high-risk and high-reward cycle of patent drugs, but how? Instead of putting on a brave face with his chairman and the board, he took the opposite tack, admitting that he needed their guidance and knowledge to find the best way forward.

He spoke to his directors, investors, and industry experts to gain a firm grasp of what would be needed in the coming years to stay competitive. As a result, Vasella in 1996 pulled off what was at the time one of the largest mergers in corporate history. He joined Sandoz with Ciba-

Geigy, Switzerland's other pharma powerhouse, to create a new enterprise based in Basel called Novartis, which at the time had annual revenue of more than $29 billion. His external circle of advisers helped him define a vision and strategy for the new company, overcome the uncertainty of merging the two cultures, and transform the new entity into one of the most innovative companies in the field.

Later in his tenure, Vasella once again reached out to a diverse group of stakeholders to help him execute his mandate. From his conversations he developed a clear view on where the industry was headed. "The applications of computing and genetics to the biomedical field were exploding," says Vasella. "At the time, we were on the verge of being able to decipher your genome for less than $1,000. We were moving to an era of so-called personalized medicine, where we will be able choose the treatment knowing the specific nature of the disease in an individual." But how to take advantage of these new developments?

Vasella reached out to his board, his team, and scientists and had his own view confirmed that some of the best breakthrough research was happening in the Boston area, especially in terms of biotechnology, and that Novartis could tap into some of the world's best talent by moving its R&D headquarters from Switzerland to Boston. His trusted team reassured him that it was not as if they were shutting down research in Basel but that they would be adding to the company's capabilities. The move would likely lead to some new areas of research and new ways of thinking. The center was a big bet; it would cost hundreds of millions, and some critics didn't want to move the company's core R&D out of Switzerland. Even so, in 2010, Vasella decided to set up a major R&D center in Cambridge, Massachusetts, a brave move for a European company that had always had its research headquarters in Switzerland. His finance team also helped guide him through the economics and the costs of opening a foreign R&D center. It was a daring move, but it turned out to be a huge success over time. The Boston lab, called the Institute of Biomedical Research, served as a model, and Novartis now has six R&D campuses around the world.

"I believe," says Vasella, "that you have to be able to express doubt to your team, a board, and other close advisers. If you don't—and you pretend—then you are playing a role, which others will sense rather easily, and that could lead to an unhealthy situation. That's not to say you should act like you're in a confessional. Facing doubt, you have to recognize if and when a decision is needed. If it is, you have to take the sword and cut through the Gordian knot and decide—despite any uncertainties. Maybe I shouldn't say it, but making a big decision also has something of gambling and playfulness to it—otherwise you'll be paralyzed by fear. You have to be able to take risks at that level without making it so personal and without taking all the burden. If you take every decision too personally, that can have a negative impact on your mental state."

One leader we know used the "not the smartest in the room" lesson to help him adapt to a new job in Asia. In 2017, Eddie Ahmed was picked to run MassMutual International, which comprised all its insurance and financial services operations outside the United States. Ahmed had a strong financial and technical background, having worked at Citigroup and Morgan Stanley. But one thing he knew was that he didn't have all the answers. So in the months after getting the job, he traveled extensively from his headquarters in Hong Kong, learning the ropes and eventually forming joint ventures in different markets to better learn the terrain.

When Ahmed took on the challenge of building MassMutual's international business, he soon realized that he needed help in navigating his way through unknown markets. He needed to become aware of what he didn't know—a tough challenge when working in multiple countries with various products and services. To do that, he created feedback loops in both his professional and personal lives. He sought out people he could reach out to whenever he had a question or a challenge, and he could be sure that they would tell him the truth and judge his ideas on a nonsubjective and impartial basis. Some of the feedback loops in the company are formal, while others are informal. Ahmed sought out people he trusted at various levels of the company as well as some from outside the company. "If I'm consistently wrong," he says, "I need to have the courage to admit that too. You must have feedback loops within your organization to give you those signals."

Even as the headwinds of geopolitics continued to make international expansion tricky, Ahmed's mindset served as an important template for future decision making. When he shared his story at the Bower Forum, the executives in the group helped him get perspective on his behavior, allowing him to more clearly define and improve his leadership style. One executive pointed out that by keeping an open mind, Ahmed, in an unbiased way, was able to take facts and then synthesize the implications and learnings. He should keep working on this skill because it would gain him personal credibility with both his executive team and the board. Another weighed in, remarking that Ahmed was doing more than sponging up information. "He had approached his conversations with his global colleagues with a different mindset that balances the long term and the short term. While taking care of quarterly earnings, he also was taking a twenty-to-fifty-year generational view, carefully weighing the opportunities as well as the risks that his company was taking. It all stemmed from Ahmed taking the long view and not getting swallowed up in the day to day."

As we saw in the two previous case studies, humility is understanding that you don't have all the answers and that if you listen deeply, you can identify and define the most crucial questions to solve or find inspiration for the answer. True listening has a yin-and-yang quality to it. On the one hand, your mind should be open enough to be receptive to the ideas of others. On the other, you must tune your attention to the specificity of what's being said.

- **Openness:** Those who can really open themselves to others live in the present moment. They create enough space for others to be heard. This starts with self-awareness and self-regulation, slowing down your inner chatter and connecting with your inner awareness (your bodily sensations, emotions, and thoughts), which allows you to be touched by others' ideas, perspectives, feelings, motivations, and intentions. Think of it as acting more authentically instead of responding through the filter of your own thoughts and emotions.

- **Tuning in:** When someone comes to you with an idea or a message, you not only have to be open to their thoughts, but you also must focus precisely on what they say. Think of it as hearing the music through all the noise in a busy bar. If you aren't focusing, someone might come to you with an idea or a message and you might miss their fear, concerns, or intentions. So bring your attention *and* tune in with precision to what others are trying to say.

How does this look in practice? At a fireside chat led by the CEO of a Fortune Global 50 company, someone asked a question. The CEO was silent for a few seconds and then, instead of directly answering, asked the questioner about the fear he sensed was underneath the question. The two then had a brief but heartfelt conversation about what was really on the questioner's mind. The facilitator of the fireside chat was so stunned by the CEO's behavior that she asked him, "Where did you go when you heard the question?" He replied, "I just received and digested the question." In other words, he was open enough to be moved by the question, and then he tuned in to what the questioner was really asking. The facilitator asked the CEO how he cultivated this quality of presence and focused attention. His reply: "I take daily walks in nature, and when I feel too stressed, I take time off to go scuba diving with my wife." As suggested by this CEO, practices of stillness, contemplation, meditation, and encounters with nature can help increase your capacity to analyze and solve problems and to interact in a human way with others.

Questions to ask yourself to become a better listener and a cultivator of ideas:

- Am I the type of person who already knows the answer before I walk into the room?

- Do I interrupt my colleagues before they have the opportunity to finish their thought?

- Do I feel calm and present or distracted and impatient when others are speaking to me?

- What is the worst that would happen if I stopped acting like I'm the smartest one in the room and opened myself up to the opinions and thoughts of others?

- Even if what I hear contradicts the way I see the world—what do I have to lose?

- How do I reconcile different ideas to produce better options and initiatives so that we conclude that the team is the "smartest in the room"?

In Summary

///

Truly being able to listen to others and actually hear what they're saying, and being able to reconcile different suggestions and ideas and then combine them in a "best of the best" thinking approach, is a key skill for leaders. We're not, however, suggesting that being a leader is like running a democracy where the idea with the most votes win. A CEO once told us that leadership is 40 percent humility and 60 percent courage. Once they've heard all sides of the argument and have reconciled different perspectives, the best leaders need to summon the confidence—based on their problem solving and judgment—to make bold decisions, while knowing that this is both a science and an art.

2

Confidence

YOU REALLY DO BELONG HERE

As the discussion got off the ground at a session of the Bower Forum, which was being held in a European capital, a young CEO sitting at the circular table gazed out the window with a distant look on his face. He seemed not only distracted but at a loss. Noticing this, one executive asked him what was on his mind. The young man, it turns out, had recently become the head of his family's business, a multibillion-dollar high-end European consumer products company. You would think anyone in that position at such an age would be thrilled and excited at the prospect of running a powerful and successful firm, but he answered, "I'm miserable and I don't know what to do."

His company's board, he explained, was a battlefield where his relatives complained about how little money they were making, had arguments over how the company should be run, and even questioned the new CEO's credentials. Such behavior made it difficult for the CEO to run the company, and he believed he had to remove some of his relatives from the board if he was to succeed at his job—a task he dreaded.

After he opened up to the group, one of the other CEOs sitting around the table said, "You've just got to deal with this. Look, they put you in this role for a reason, and the board obviously has confidence in you. You have to find the courage to overcome your lack of confidence by figuring out what's keeping you back and confronting it." This simple observation helped the young CEO realize that he feared upsetting his relatives but that it was more important to do what was right for the business. This lifted his sense of dread and gave him the courage to act. Said one executive present, "It was like watching a caterpillar turn into a butterfly." The group then hashed out an ingenious solution. The company had a long-standing family council that had been underutilized, and the CEO decided to make that the forum for his family's concerns. There they could air their personal grievances outside of the board meetings. It worked beautifully. The family felt valued, and the CEO was able to keep their personal issues out of the boardroom.

When leaders struggle—as in the case of our European CEO—it is sometimes because they lack the confidence to act. They don't feel they have the power to push new ideas or set bold new directions for the organization or perform to the best of their ability. And without the will and fortitude to execute their mandate, they often fail. Our second element of leadership—confidence—asks leaders to overcome their uncertainty by taking a hard and unbiased look at themselves to find their weaknesses and then change.

History is rife with examples of people who summoned the inner courage to overcome obstacles and thrive in places where they felt they didn't belong. Ellen MacArthur, one of the world's top offshore sailors, had to overcome her fears and uncertainties to achieve her dreams. Growing up in landlocked Derbyshire as the daughter of two schoolteachers, she was not someone who seemed to belong in the elite and highly competitive world of ocean racing. She recalls watching a sailing program on TV when she was seventeen and saying to herself, "That's what I'm going to do." As unlikely as that journey seemed, MacArthur felt that she belonged to that world because she had a passion for sailing, and she told herself that she *could* sail around the world. "I think the fundamental thing," she says, "is knowing that you absolutely want to achieve something. I was very lucky at the age of seventeen to be able to say: 'That's where I'm going.' If you don't know where you want to go, you can't have that same level of motivation." She went on to become one of the most accomplished sailors in the world. In 2005, she broke the record for circumnavigating the globe.

Lynn Elsenhans, a Bower Forum coach who was the former CEO of the oil company Sunoco and now sits on the boards of Baker Hughes and Saudi Aramco, is a great example of someone who overcame her insecurities of being a woman in a predominantly male world. When she started her career at Royal Dutch Shell in Houston, she was the only woman in an office of fifty men. She thrived by preparing herself mentally every day. She says that "many women have what's termed impostor syndrome, where they feel they don't belong. The thing that helped me tremendously is that I always persuaded myself that I did indeed belong." To do that, Elsenhans drew on her educational background whenever she felt insecure. She had majored in applied mathematics at Rice and earned a Harvard MBA. "I had an education that was as good as that of any of the men in the room."

Even so, she faced some trying times. In such a male-dominated world, she had to confront numerous microaggressions and slights. Whether consciously or not, some men would treat her as the little lady in the room. One time, a manager, assuming that she was an executive assistant, turned to her and asked her to get him a cup of coffee. Elsenhans could have snapped at him to get his own, but she took a different, and to her mind a more humble, approach. She calmly replied, "I'd be very happy to do that, and the next time it's your turn." Her response defused the situation while at the same time allowing Elsenhans to get the message across that she was on equal footing.

In another instance, Elsenhans, who at the time was running Shell's multibillion-dollar solvents business, received an invitation to attend a conference at the company's London headquarters. When she arrived, she was the only woman, and even though the business she ran was much larger than those of some of the men at the conference, her title was junior to theirs. That meant that she technically wasn't allowed to eat in the dining room for top execs. But she showed up anyway. One of the Shell executives sidled up to her at the bar and said, "Nobody approves of you being here. You should be at home with your kids and with your husband." Although Elsenhans's first thought was to tell him to go to hell, instead she gathered her confidence and calmly said, "Thank you for sharing that. I just really hadn't thought about that." The executive hadn't expected that reaction and started up a meaningful conversation with her. "It's all about holding your ground," says Elsenhans. "It is having the confidence to know you do belong there and not apologizing for being there, but also not being too aggressive. Keep it light." The key is to find your authentic self.

Not all men, of course, looked down on Elsenhans. In fact, later in her career, some of her colleagues felt resentful of her success. With her degrees from prestigious universities, her reputation for being a quick and tough analytical thinker, and her impressive work habits, some of her colleagues felt intimidated. At the time, Shell was trying to foster diversity, and some felt that Elsenhans got promoted over them because she was a woman. "Once I became self-aware enough to know that I intimidated people," she recalls, "I spent a lot of time trying to make those I intimidated feel comfortable about their own abilities. A big part of my job was to make both men and women more confident by believing in them and believing that they are capable of doing things that they don't think they're capable of doing." She learned this lesson from one of her mentors at Shell who had believed in her. He put his reputation on the line by recommending Elsenhans for a key job in the company's manufacturing division even though she didn't have an engineering degree. Other executives wanted her to go into the finance department, but Elsenhans felt that would have thrown her off the track for running an operating unit, an important stepping-stone to becoming a CEO. At the refinery she was assigned to, she discovered an operating improvement that ended up saving the company $10,000 a day—a lot of money in 1992. Never forgetting what her mentor did for her, she did all she could through the rest of her career to develop and support those around her. She helped herself by helping them.

Confidence can also play an important role in one's career trajectory. Elsenhans has seen that at times young executives—especially women—might lack the confidence to push for the next promotion. Some hold themselves back, fearing they don't have what it takes to do the job. Young executives need the courage to take those tough, demanding jobs—perhaps even moving their families overseas for a period—if they want to stay on the CEO track. "If you want to be a CEO," says Elsenhans, "you need to take the assignments—even if it means going backward—that get you the building blocks of what the board is looking for in a CEO."

What many young executives don't understand, she says, is that the best new job opportunities are designed to stretch one's abilities. No one is expected to get everything right immediately. These jobs have a learning curve, but in the long run they foster new skills, and the bosses giving out those career-making jobs don't expect anyone to figure them out right off the bat. "If you're thinking of taking a challenging new job," says Elsenhans, "you should ask yourself what's the worst thing that could happen to you. If you make a mistake, chances are your boss will just tell you not to do it again. It's better to beg for forgiveness than to ask for permission."

As Elsenhans discovered, being a woman in a man's world has its challenges. That's doubly compounded when you're a woman of color working in Silicon Valley. Anju Patwardhan, a fintech VC, used a simple tool to navigate her way through male-dominated cultures. As a successful fintech fund executive, Patwardhan meets powerful people from all around the world. She travels constantly and sits on many boards, including one at a Saudi bank as a nominee of the sovereign wealth fund. The investing world is notoriously masculine, and as an Indian woman, she sometimes felt invisible. Often male executives would assume that she was a junior staffer. The fact that she kept her own calendar as a VC so she could better manage her affairs across multiple time zones signaled to them that she couldn't have much power. After all, she was a woman and must not have her own assistant. "If I attended a meeting with a white male," recalls Patwardhan, "somehow people would assume that the white male was the boss." She had a workaround, however. She created a long, detailed profile that highlighted her accomplishments as a former top banker at Citicorp and Standard Chartered and her stellar academic career and global awards. Roughly twenty-four hours before every meeting, her assistant sent it to the people she was going to meet. "I realized that from the time I started doing it, the conversations changed," she says. "The people I was going to meet would read my profile beforehand, and then I was treated as an equal or better than an equal."

Patwardhan, however, did not gain her sense of belonging simply from male executives treating her as an equal. It was because she took agency. She assumed that she belonged in the first place and showed up at her meetings in a way that created that reality. She was not a victim but approached situations with the mindset of "I belong." Out of this mindset, she took action to manifest her reality. The point is, you already won. You have a seat at the table, so take it! (You'll learn more about Patwardhan later in the book.)

Time and again we've heard from leaders who feel at a loss when they suddenly find themselves working internationally. In many cases they don't know the language, the culture, or the business rules of engagement. They don't feel like they belong. They don't have the courage to act. Where do you start, how do you know you really understand what's going on, and how can you adapt to the culture in a short amount of time?

Ford's Mark Fields faced that very dilemma when in 1998 the company asked him to move to Japan to work for Mazda. (Ford at the time owned one-third of the car company.) The first thing Fields did when he arrived in Japan was to obtain some cultural literacy. He spent the first six months speaking with colleagues in Japan, reading books on Japanese management, and getting out as much as possible so he could get a feel for the land and its people. "I knew if I had walked in as an American with guns blazing," he recalls, "and said, 'Here's the plan,' I would fail."

Ford Motor sent Fields to Japan because Mazda was in trouble. With bankruptcy a possibility, Fields was tempted to move quickly, but from what he had learned about Japanese culture, he concluded that rushing a ninety-day turnaround plan wasn't the best approach. "Companies in Japan tend to be very siloed," he says, "so if the manufacturing head does their job, they think the company should be successful. If the CFO does their job, the company should be successful. But no one really understood how the company made money."

During his first four or five months as CEO, Fields spent two weekends each month with his management team, just immersing them in the business. "This was a shock to the Japanese managers," he says, "because in Mazda's culture, if you were a managing director of finance or manufacturing, you were a statesman who didn't get into details." Fields had also picked up that the concept of legacy was very important to the Japanese, so he told them, "We could argue about how we got into this bad situation, but playing the victim card is not the exciting thing to do. Instead, think about what legacy you want to leave for the next generation of employees." Fields also learned that Japanese culture could be very insular, so he brought in experts from outside the country to talk about the global auto market. Eventually he began to win his team's commitment to the new turnaround plan. By the end of those off-sites, the strategy had switched from being the "Fields plan" to the "Mazda plan."

One of the words Fields learned early on in Japan was *nemawashi*, which means planting seeds. At first he didn't understand the concept, but then it dawned on him: If he were to implement a successful turnaround plan, it would have to be designed in a way that brought the executive team along. That, however, would take time and patience. "I'm a type-A person," says Fields. "Right? So, I wanted to start executing. I really had to throttle myself, and there were days I wanted to put my head through the wall." When Fields would fly back to Ford headquarters in Michigan, the top brass would ask him what was taking so long. Fields explained to them that in Japanese culture, executives take an extended period to develop the plan and strategy, but then the execution is quicker because everyone owns the plan. In the West, the tendency is to quickly sign off on the plan and then take a longer time trying to drag everyone along. The Japanese approach seems longer, but it's actually quicker, he argued.

Although he was an outsider, Fields found another way to make himself belong at the Japanese company. He worked hard to understand how personal relationships worked in Japan. There, a confrontational style is frowned upon. The Japanese fear losing face. Yet when Fields arrived, he found that the CFO he had inherited, who was a transplanted Ford employee, was smart and capable but seemed to be rubbing his Japanese colleagues the wrong way. His aggressive style was alienating many at the automaker. As a new CEO, Fields at first was reluctant to move, but he finally replaced the CFO with another executive from Ford who had already earned a lot of respect from the Japanese. "When I look back on my career," says Fields, "I never felt in retrospect that I moved too fast on a person who wasn't a good fit. When I pulled the ripcord on my CFO, it changed the whole tenor of the management team. Once the Japanese knew I had listened and was serious about changing the place, the whole team became more open to the process."

Often at the Bower Forum, a CEO would share with others that they felt they didn't have the necessary industry expertise or relevant functional expertise to run their organization. They were good leaders with a successful track record, but they were surrounded by experts in software, AI, engineering, or medicine who made the core of the company tick. "I didn't really feel I belonged there," said one.

That's the challenge Michael Fisher faced when he became the CEO of the nonprofit Cincinnati Children's Hospital Medical Center in 2010. "I'm leading an academic medical center as the CEO—and I was not a physician, not a scientist, not a nurse, and didn't spend my career in that field," he recalls. He worked hard to further build his credibility and confidence running this organization, which treats nearly 1.7 million patients every year, by listening, partnering, and trying to closely understand the needs of those patients and their families, as well as the doctors, nurses, and researchers who worked there. Under Fisher, Cincinnati Children's became even more successful, but after a few years at the job, he felt he and the institution could be even better. He grew concerned that he couldn't initiate some major changes that he thought would enable the organization to reach its fullest potential.

"We were doing well on all the patient care, research, and financial metrics," says Fisher, "but I knew I wasn't clicking on all cylinders yet. I wasn't sure that I belonged, that I was a highly capable CEO for this large, complex enterprise." Fisher shared with his colleagues at the Bower Forum his insecurities and his fear that he didn't have the right skills and support to unleash a bolder transformation agenda for the medical center. "As we went through the formal sessions and during the breaks and meals, I remember this growing sense from my peers that they wanted me to get over myself and be more ambitious. One coach, who was the former head of a Fortune Global 50 company, said to Fisher, "What you need is a kick in the butt! The clock is ticking, and you have to get much more intentional about what you're going to get done in the remaining few years of your tenure."

Coming out of the Bower Forum, Fisher felt energized. Before long he changed several players on his senior team and began more deeply investing in not only his own but also each team member's individual leadership capabilities as well as the functioning and chemistry of the team as a whole. As Fisher learned, to have a sense of belonging means having a healthy self-esteem both for yourself and your team that is grounded in a belief that you are worthy of those you work with—not only for what you do but for who you are and your particular strengths.

When he returned to his job from the forum, Fisher's aspirations for the organization rose significantly. Years earlier, he had helped form a network of children's hospitals to partner on improving patient safety. Now newly energized, Fisher doubled down on the project, and by the time he left his CEO job more than 140 children's hospitals across North America had joined the network. As board chair of the effort, Fisher encouraged them not to compete on safety metrics but to work together by sharing data and best practices. As a result, twenty thousand children avoided serious harm from medical errors over a ten-year period, while the health care system saved hundreds of millions of dollars. A couple of years after he was inspired at the Bower Forum, Fisher elevated his commitment on pediatric and adolescent mental health. This included a $100 million investment in a reimagined mental health facility and a dramatic increase in research and institutional partnerships for mental health. "In the end," says Fisher, "it was all about strengthening my confidence and leveraging my unique value, skills, and leadership that I did have."

Belonging is a birthright. When you experience an inherent sense of belonging, it means you have a healthy sense of who you are. You feel safe to take personal risks, admit mistakes, ask for support, make tough decisions even when they are unpopular, and invite collaboration. Next time you face a challenging decision or situation, ask yourself, "If I believed that I belong (versus a need to prove myself, be right, be the smartest, or do it alone), how would I approach this situation or decision?" Would you make a decision to prove you belong in this role or for the good of the organization? This approach will likely change not only the decision you make but also how you make it, by engaging more voices without giving away your right to make the final decision.

Questions to ask yourself to strengthen your sense of belonging:

//

- What rational and emotional reasons are essential for me to stay at this organization?

- Would the board have chosen me if they didn't believe I could do the job?

- Am I learning the right skills to keep up with the ever-evolving demands of my job?

- Do I feel safe to take personal risks, admit mistakes, invite collaboration, make tough decisions even when they are unpopular? If not, what is making me feel that way?

- If I believed that I belong (as opposed to acting out of a need to prove myself, be right, or do it alone), how would I approach this situation or decision differently?

//

In Summary

//

The best leaders develop a sense of true belonging by convincing themselves that they are indeed the right person for the job even if they're harboring some insecurities. They find the courage to overcome their lack of confidence by figuring out what's keeping them back and confronting it. They are also open to frank feedback from those around them so they can learn how to contribute in meaningful ways. It is not about the need to be superior or loved by others but rather about having a shared sense of belonging, anchored in a shared courage to make decisions even if they are unpopular or come with some personal risk. But in an uncertain world, how do you know what's the right decision? In the next chapter we examine in more depth whether you're making a decision for the good of the organization or for your own personal glory or a desire to be liked.

3

STOP TRYING TO PROVE YOURSELF

One CEO attending a Bower Forum in Florida felt frustrated about the lack of progress he was making at his software company. "I have a great strategy and what I think is a good team, but when I lead the charge, I look back and no one is following me." After some frank discussion about the young leader's style, it became increasingly clear that he was insecure about his position, which made him feel like he needed to prove himself to others. Instead of opening himself to diverse opinions and changing his mind when his colleagues had a better idea, he had a fixed mindset where he always had to have the answers and he always had to be right. After all, wasn't he the CEO? Shouldn't he have all the answers?

One coach, a seasoned CEO, challenged him. "It's a disease that's all too common," she said. "Your ego gives you a false sense of superiority, which drives a wedge between you and your team. You have to switch from proving yourself to thinking about what's best for the organization. Rather than a fixed mindset, have a flexible mindset where, when the facts warrant it, you can change your mind and put your organization ahead of your ego. Don't try to prove yourself and show the world how great you are. If you want your team and your company to become more and more effective, you need to put your ego on a shelf." The coach hit on the head the gist of our third element of leadership, "Selflessness."

Having an ego is not in itself a bad thing. All leaders need a well-developed self-image. But problems can arise when leaders have an inflated ego, which leads to grandiosity. An outsized ego sometimes stems from a need to prove yourself to someone, be it your parents, your spouse, your colleagues, or even yourself. It is a powerful force that can keep you from being your best self. At work, ego can trigger bad behavior, such as office politics, self-promotion, and arrogance, traits that cause others not to want to collaborate closely with you. The goal is to develop a healthy ego, rooted in healthy self-esteem. Our third element of leadership, selflessness, entails learning to recognize when you're acting out of an inflated sense of self, and if you are, squashing this tendency by putting the good of the organization ahead of your own glory.

We've found that when making major decisions excellent CEOs think about values first. They tell themselves that they're here to create value not for themselves but for the organization or system they're serving. The concept of servant leadership has been well documented, but from our experience, few know how to subjugate their egos to the greater good. The best ask themselves, "Is this the right decision for the organization, for our people, for the purpose of this organization, or is it my ego that is driving me? Am I making this decision because I am thinking of my credibility, trying to save face, or reacting to what the next article in the press might say about me? Or is it because it is truly the right thing to do?"

The best leaders have the confidence to listen to others knowing that it does not put their credibility into question. In fact, it's quite the opposite. Having listened to all stakeholders and perspectives, they have the confidence to drive the right decision, not the popular decision—not the one that is consensus driven or tailored to please stakeholders. They are willing to change their mind when appropriate based on what they hear from others. They are ready to move ahead even in those circumstances when the course of action is unclear. You should ask yourself what part of you is making the decision. Is it the creative, bold, passionate, and excited you? Or the one avoiding conflict? Looking for approval?

History provides examples of people who succeeded by setting their egos aside in pursuit of a greater good. Mahatma Gandhi often eschewed wealth and power and even placed his health and life at risk as he led nonviolent resistance to British rule in India. Nelson Mandela, despite being imprisoned for twenty-seven years by the South African government, never lost sight of his goal of ending apartheid and eventually rose to lead the nation.

In the United States, perhaps the most notable example of a selfless leader is U.S. president Abraham Lincoln. His willingness to put the needs of the country ahead of accruing personal power ultimately helped him to preserve the Union and end slavery. In her book *Team of Rivals*, historian Doris Kearns Goodwin explains how during the Civil War Lincoln chose a number of fierce political rivals to serve in his cabinet, including William H. Seward, Salmon P. Chase, and Edward Bates, who had for years strongly opposed the president and his views. Instead of appointing yes-men, Lincoln put his ego aside and reached out to the best minds that he could find. He knew he couldn't lead America alone through the biggest crisis it had ever faced. He needed cabinet members with diverse views, and he had the humility to encourage debate, to listen, and, if necessary, to change his mind.

In contrast to these great historical figures, many CEOs spend too much energy trying to prove how great they are instead of getting the job done as effectively and productively as possible, and are more obsessed with self-glorification than with creating value for the company. That's exactly what the CEO of a troubled Swiss financial firm discovered in the midst of what turned out to be a successful turnaround.

As with many things in life, timing is everything. That was especially true when Bruno Pfister, who had been the CFO of the financial firm Swiss Life, was appointed CEO just a few months before the Lehman Brothers crisis of 2008. With the collapse of Lehman, the financial world went into meltdown mode. Liquidity for almost all financial instruments vanished and credit spreads exploded, so that the investment portfolios of companies such as Swiss Life took a beating, with many suffering paper losses in the billions. Like many top leaders during this financial crisis, Pfister felt stressed and unsure of which steps to take and in which order to first stabilize and then turn around his struggling company.

To navigate through such a difficult personal journey, Pfister relied in part on advice that he got from a trusted mentor. "The issue," the CEO says, "is to find somebody you can turn to on both critical business matters and very personal issues, because when you are at the top, you feel lonely. In our conservative culture in Western Europe a person like that is not so easy to find, but it's worth the effort."

His mentor told him one thing in particular that at the time struck Pfister as odd. He said, "Bruno, you need to think about what kind of legacy you want to leave to your successor." Pfister replied with exasperation: "Are you mad? I'm in the midst of a crisis. I was just appointed CEO, and I'm not thinking about leaving." Pfister at first felt that his mentor had asked the wrong question and therefore ignored his advice. However, the idea kept coming back to him over the following months. It caused him to revise his picture of what the company should look like after he leaves, not just in terms of financials and key performance metrics but also in terms of Swiss Life's corporate culture, attitudes and behavior, decision-making processes, and the way people communicate and cooperate with one another.

The culture he pictured was one where employees more rigorously analyzed the balance sheet and profit and loss statement, understood more thoroughly product and channel profitability, moved faster when the situation required, sped up product development, and took the initiative within the bounds of what regulations and internal rules allowed. In other words, he wanted Swiss Life's conservative, slow-moving culture to be more entrepreneurial, more decisive, with an increased focus on customer needs and generally faster moving. He set out to establish a consistent set of metrics and behaviors all aimed at achieving that transformation.

Pfister had his work cut out for him, as he discovered one Sunday afternoon when he was working at home during the early weeks of the turnaround. He had two new directives on his desk from different departments using inconsistent terminology and partly contradicting each other. In fact, he didn't even fully understand them. On Monday he called his executive staff together and told them they had to "clean up the framework of internal rules and regulations by clarifying what needs to be regulated internally, creating a simple hierarchical rule structure, and ensuring that one subject matter is only treated once." This system was first implemented at the group level and then pushed down to each reporting level. Within the entire organization it created clarity regarding who individually or collectively was responsible to make which kinds of decisions. This helped orient the entire staff to the right people or committees, decisions began to be made much faster, and erratic upward delegation disappeared quite quickly.

Once Pfister created a clear visual picture in his mind of how the company should look in the future, his self-confidence and decision making significantly improved. "The mental vision became a compass," he says. "I started to systematically approve those requests that helped implement my vision; on the other hand, I turned down every request compromising the vision, and I supported neutral requests, if they brought the business forward."

Despite his desire to build a more entrepreneurial organization, Pfister believed that Swiss Life should run on a centralized model. This belief resulted from his prior professional experiences and observations. Of course, the workers beneath him could still take more initiative, but the CEO needed to be closely involved in the running of the company's business units.

When Pfister started to request concrete steps toward centralization, he got hard pushback from some of his best managers. How could they be more entrepreneurial if they as local leaders did not control all elements of the business anymore? Why and for what benefit should corporate have to approve every move? As Pfister listened carefully to the various arguments and considerations, he began to think they had real merit. Yet historically, CEOs were supposed to be the voice of authority; they were supposed to be right all the time. This is especially so in Swiss organizations, which are known for their top-down approaches.

"If I'm honest and frank with myself," says Pfister, "there was a moment where I thought that if I changed my mind, it could threaten my position or my influence, undermine my authority, or cause people to respect me less. I went to a quiet room and tested what I'd feel like if I admitted I was wrong. I realized that my concerns had more to do with my ego than the good of the organization and its DNA. It was more of an egotistical kind of fear I had than an institutional one. The interesting thing was that the pushback came from different leaders, some of whom I had known for many years, respected, and trusted a lot. I concluded that it would actually help strengthen my authority, position, and influence to show that I listened and took the view of the team."

Pfister swallowed his pride and told his team that they were indeed right. After that moment of truth, he and his team went about instilling into the culture consequential decentralized decision making within a clear framework of very strong functional leadership. For example, he pushed down some IT resources to the business unit so that it could be more responsive to its needs. Pfister told the manager that to be able to pay for the IT he'd have to save 40 percent of the costs over the next three years. Having been given the freedom to act, the unit manager said, "I'll figure out a way to do it!" In less than two years the excess costs were gone.

Of course, those who didn't buy into the decentralized model and the new culture of discipline and speed were asked to leave. "We needed to find employees," says Pfister, "who could cooperate in a way where all their skills and all their talents were utilized in the best possible way." To find the right people with the right attitudes and mindsets, Pfister focused on the top hundred of his over ten-thousand-person workforce. Together with his executive team, he moved about a third of them to new positions, replaced a third of the managers from the outside, and only the remaining third had the same job eighteen months later.

By putting the organization ahead of his ego, Pfister began to see some real value creation. The organization became less political and more efficient. People started acting like owners rather than order takers. Says Pfister, "I appealed to personal accountability, personal responsibility, and whatever they had to do or decide, I asked them to always do it in the best, most economic way in the interest of the company. To put it more simply: I asked the employees to act as if they owned the company."

By the spring of 2013, just four years after Pfister started his cultural transformation, his visual picture of how Swiss Life should look became reality. Not only did the company generate returns exceeding its cost of capital, but life changed for the CEO. He says that he was able to cut his workweek from over a hundred hours to sixty, the number of emails in his inbox dropped by half, his assistant, who had threatened to quit because of the workload, was asking for more assignments, and the position of chief of staff could be eliminated when he quit the company in 2014. As of 2022, Pfister's legacy remained rock solid. Swiss Life reported all-time record profits.

When an organization's strategy needs to change, it's often not easy to make the shift. You probably spent a lot of time, resources, and personal prestige on the old strategy, and suddenly admitting that the company now needs a new direction or shift in focus is not easy to swallow. You might fear that by abandoning or adjusting your current plan you'll lose influence in the eyes of your employees, or that they'll see you as confused or indecisive. Even so, it's better for leaders to put their egos aside and embrace the new plan. A selfless leader would not ask themselves, "How did I build my own reputation in this role?" Rather, they would ask themselves, "What organization did I leave behind? Who are the leaders that I developed? Did I lead the organization to new heights and make the decisions that were right for it—sometimes at my own expense?"

To take the sting out of changing course, it helps to have a method for making decisions that ensures the organization's values are being upheld and justifies the need for change. In that way, if a change of heart becomes necessary and the new decision fits with the organization's cultural values, people will be more willing to understand and accept the change.

When Gonzalve Bich, a Bower Forum attendee and the CEO of BIC, the world's leading maker of stationery, lighters, and shavers, and the grandson of the company's founder, took over from his father in 2018, he inherited a company that needed to be reorganized and refreshed. Although BIC is a public company, the Bich family controls 63 percent of the voting rights. So the young CEO not only had outside investors to please but also a large number of family members, some of whom worked at the company. The stock had been slipping and the challenge was to make relevant a company that made disposable products in an era when sustainability was becoming ever more important to consumers.

Earlier in his career at BIC, Bich, who had run operations in various spots around the globe, had become overwhelmed by decision making. "There was too much data," he says. "You'd sit in a room watching a three-hundred-slide PowerPoint, which was slickly put together, but by the end of the presentation, you'd have no idea what the point of it all was." Out of necessity, he created a simplified decision-making process that has served him well as CEO because it was based on doing what was good for the company rather than on his personal biases or mounds of confusing data.

As a student of history at Harvard, Bich recalled how American president Woodrow Wilson used to make decisions at the White House. Wilson would ask for an executive summary of the issue, form a hypothesis, and then talk to no fewer than three and no more than five trusted experts inside and outside the White House before making a decision. Drawing inspiration from Wilson's method, Bich crafted a new approach and methodology, and saved himself countless hours with improved decision making.

Even so, decision making was still tough for him. Sometimes a decision, even though it seemed rational, didn't feel right. "You end up awake late one night at two-thirty in the morning and you have five decisions in front of you, and they've been piling up and piling up," says Bich. "You've been reading the reports and doing math and calling the experts, and you're sitting there, and you say to yourself, 'I just need to decide because that's what stands between me and a few hours of sleep.' I could spend another hour worrying, but I'm not sure the decision would be better and that's an hour of sleep I'll lose. I will need that energy tomorrow to give a speech, negotiate, or whatever."

The best leaders not only learn to be selfless and overcome their egos, but they also institutionalize a process to do so. To make his life (and his nights) a bit less stressful and his decisions more understandable to his team, Bich devised three ethical principles to guide every decision he makes. That helps ensure that every decision is for the organization's good rather than for salving the CEO's ego. Making decisions that way, Bich says, helps him have a good feeling about them, and has made him more effective, lowering his fail rate. "So, instead of making those decisions in the middle of the night, I'm making them at six in the evening, and then I go home and make dinner for the kids. I have a good night."

To come up with his three principles, he visualized being sixty-five, sitting in his rocking chair surrounded by nature and thinking back to the decisions he made as CEO. "Am I going to feel good as a person about it? If the answer is anything other than a resounding yes, I'll find another way."

So, for every decision he makes, Bich asks himself three questions: Does it create value? Does it create opportunities? Is it a force for good? Value is not just financial. It could be a move that strengthens the long-term outlook for the company but costs the bottom line in the short run. Opportunity can mean, will the decision create a new business or generate new jobs? Finally, will the decision be good for the community? Will it exacerbate climate change or mitigate it? Will it create more waste or less? Will it lead to more diversity of thought? As Bich explains,

"In my life I chose not to do public service. I chose not to be a painter or a poet—I've no artistic ability. But if I can do my job in such a way that it's a force for good, I sleep well at night."

Even though Bich created a robust framework for making decisions that allowed him to act quickly and with conviction, he sometimes found that in the heat of the moment he would ignore his own rules and go by his gut—a behavior he sometimes would regret. When Bich decided to reorganize the company shortly after he became CEO in 2019, he knew what he wanted to do: centralize. He planned to switch the global company from a decentralized structure, run by category and market, to a functionally led business with centralized centers of excellence to pool resources and share know-how, while also scaling the business in terms of future M&A. His idea was to encourage more of an entrepreneurial mindset.

"At that point, I was 80 percent convinced that it was the right thing to do, but I was still fighting it because I have an ego and I just didn't want to be wrong. My team said, 'Okay, but we don't have time. You need to just make your call.'" Bich, who takes pride in making fast decisions, apologized to his team, and then did something he rarely did—he postponed it one for a week to think about it more. By the end of the week, he decided to move forward with centralization. What changed his mind? Bich realized that he had ignored his decision-making method, so he reached out to one more expert who hadn't been privy to any of the debate, trials and tribulations, and arguments over the issue. "In two days," says Bich, "he was able to help me unlock my thinking. That's amazing."

Ultimately, his tried-and-true decision-making process had led him to the right decision—one that was best for his organization, not his ego.

*Questions to ask yourself to find out
if you're acting out of ego rather than
for the good of the organization:*

//

- What part of me is making the decision? Is it the creative, bold, passionate, and excited me or the me who avoids conflict and looks for approval?

- Am I making a decision that has more to do with my own reputation and ego than that of the organization I will leave behind?

- How and when am I willing to change my mind based on what I hear from others?

- Do I have the confidence to listen to others without feeling my credibility is being questioned?

- Having listened to all stakeholders and perspectives, do I have the confidence to drive the right decision, not the popular decision—not the one that is consensus driven or tailored to please stakeholders?

- How and when am I willing to change my mind based on what I hear from others?

- How do I know that my assumptions and beliefs are wrong or need to be changed, and that I need to objectively look at different and better options?

//

In Summary

///

Many leaders at the top struggle with decision making not because the decisions are inherently hard to make but because the leaders do not have healthy confidence and strong self-esteem. Think of some decisions you made recently that may not have led to the desired outcomes or the level of commitment you wanted from your team. Did you make them because you needed to be seen as the one who has the right answer, knows better, and appears strong and confident? Despite your best intentions, did you let your ego get in the way at the cost of engaging others, seeking opposing voices, or asking how you might be wrong? Worse still, did you make it from a sense of wanting to be liked, conforming to expectations, or pleasing too many stakeholders?

As we've seen, making decisions based on the good of the organization—focusing on those objectives or priorities that drive your company's success—is the ultimate selflessness. Being able to go beyond your own sense of self to achieve what is best for the team, the organization, and the world around you is critical to being successful—this is the ultimate definition of selfless leadership. But how can you ensure that you're getting the best thoughts and insight from colleagues, advisers, and friends? That's where vulnerability plays a huge role.

4

Vulnerability

IT'S OKAY TO BE YOURSELF

O n a rainy day in Paris, the handful of CEOs gathered at the Bower Forum were surprised by the depth of anguish coming from one of their own. After all, this person was a highly successful leader of a family-owned global manufacturing firm who had a reputation for maintaining strong bonds with his board, his management team, and his outside constituents. "My problem," he said to those around the table, "is that I can't confront people." He went on to explain how one of his relatives, who was on his leadership team, was strutting around the place like he owned it—which, of course, he did in part. The executive was a negative influence, saying, "This person was an idiot, that one was useless, or that other one was undercutting him behind his back." The CEO knew he had to confront this person, but he couldn't gather the courage.

One of the CEOs at the table asked him why he felt that way. After some soul-searching conversation, the CEO realized that he was raised by his mother in a way that made him want to please everyone. He said he never had a deep relationship with his mother. Each time he came to her with a problem, she said, "Oh, this is not a problem. This will be resolved. Don't worry." The family never argued at dinner, were always polite and deferential with one another. His ability to play ambassador helped him forge strong ties with his directors and his other constituents, but it also let him down when it came to confronting someone like the relative who was acting aggressively. Once he realized the root causes for his behavior, he gained more confidence. Just because his mother wanted him to please everyone didn't mean he had to act that way. After the CEO returned to work, he confronted his relative, telling him that in the end it might be better if he looked outside for a new opportunity, and to the CEO's relief the person eventually left the company without making a fuss.

As we can see from this case, making themselves vulnerable in order to get in touch with their feelings can change the way leaders deal with often unrecognized patterns that were established earlier in their lives. This includes how they were brought up and were shaped by their parents, their teachers, and their bosses early in their careers. As one seasoned CEO put it, "There is no deep learning without emotional involvement." That's an idea that often meets resistance. Another executive we know shared a big challenge facing his company when we asked him how he felt about it. "Why does it matter how I feel?" he replied. "I'm an engineer. We're trained to see facts, not emotions."

A crucial aspect of the fourth element of our leadership process is learning to be vulnerable in certain situations. Many see this as a sign of weakness, whereas it is in fact a sign of strength. When handled correctly, vulnerability is power. The image of the stoic leader is ingrained in our collective psyche as the default model. You're not supposed to show your emotions at the office or get involved with people on a human level. You're the boss, you're in charge, and you can't show weakness or vulnerability.

Yet that's not the model that motivates workers in today's world. Millennials especially want their leaders to be authentic, to share their human side, including vulnerabilities. Otherwise, this generation tends to clam up, mentally drop out, or, worse yet, leave their jobs for another they believe will be more fulfilling. Acting like everything you do has to be perfect and always trying to prove that you are a superhuman leader will destroy good teamwork and distance people from you. Instead, you need to switch from proving to improving yourself. Rather than a fixed mindset, have an open, more authentic mindset where you believe you can always do better. To connect with others, you need to bring your true self to work and to each situation you face, focusing on personal growth rather than perception management. You must be willing to take risks, to invest in relationships that may or may not work out, and to act with no guarantees. You need to be vulnerable.

Vulnerability is about the willingness to be touched by others' emotions, perspectives, and stories while at the same time allowing yourself to be seen fully by others. When you let yourself be vulnerable, you share your greatest strengths, hopes, dreams, concerns, anxieties, and questions—even if you fear being judged. Contrary to conventional wisdom, vulnerability is not a weakness. It can be magnetic and powerful.

Some of the toughest, most autocratic business leaders knew the value of being vulnerable. Few entrepreneurs dominated their company the way Apple's Steve Jobs did, yet later in his career he learned the importance of being authentic and sharing his thoughts and emotions with others. Jobs, who struggled with health problems throughout his life, including pancreatic cancer, openly talked about his struggles with cancer and his mortality in his famous 2005 Stanford commencement speech: "Remembering that I'll be dead soon is the most important tool I've ever encountered to help me make the big choices in life." His openness added to his reputation as one of the most remarkable entrepreneurs who ever lived.

If you want to be trusted, you need to show your vulnerability. The challenge facing us all is exactly when to open ourselves up and when to keep a stiff upper lip. You probably don't want to be vulnerable during a big board meeting, but it might make more sense when you're gathered with colleagues to tackle a tough problem. The ultimate purpose of being vulnerable is that it gives you permission to invite thoughts and insights from colleagues, advisers, and friends. If you put up a defensive wall around you, if you act secretively, people aren't likely to relate to you. Plus, if you want to build trust in your organization, you should teach your executive team also to be open—as we'll explore more deeply in part 2 of this book. Remember that the research shows the number one reason teams fail is a lack of trust.

Vulnerability has a lot to do with managing our triggers. A trigger is something that causes us to respond emotionally. It could be something someone says or does, or it could be a situation or a challenge. Triggers in and of themselves aren't positive or negative. What they do is spark fear in us. A trigger could be one of your team members constantly engaging in toxic behavior, or it could be an activist knocking at your door, a board member making a snarky comment about the latest quarterly results, or even the governor of your state attacking you for being woke.

If leaders do not know their own triggers, they get trapped by their own patterns, which can lead to negative behavior and poor performance. The danger is reacting quickly in the moment and reverting to old patterns that can make us want to control the situation or defend our ego rather than do what's best for the business. Fortunately, we have the choice of responding to our triggers either positively or negatively. The best leaders recognize what is triggering them and then learn to respond to the situation in an open and positive way.

This is where vulnerability comes into play. If some trigger forces you to react negatively or defensively, and you're able to realize that's what's happening, you can change your behavior by asking yourself or by discussing with others why you're reacting in such a way—in other words, by leaning into your vulnerability in order to recognize your triggers. You're allowing yourself to be touched. It's important as we lean into vulnerability to cultivate a deep self-awareness so that we can catch ourselves in a moment of reactivity and be able to pause and respond in positive, creative ways. Being vulnerable in this way means that a leader is trying to master the five balancing acts, which, as we explained in the introduction of this book, include moving from control to collaboration and from competition to cocreation.

Sometimes, understanding what's triggering you requires you to take a deep look inside yourself. Whenever she was at a board meeting, a new CEO got triggered by a director who she felt didn't know what she was talking about. Every time the CEO heard something she thought was wrong or naïve, she would jump in to correct the director—which made for awkward meetings. After some deep self-reflection, the CEO realized that the problem was she felt she had to be seen as being right all the time. She realized that she was reverting to her childhood pattern of being the kid who always had the answer. The CEO felt that the director was competing with her, threatening her identity. It triggered a fear in her that had nothing to do with the present moment or what was good for the business, but everything to do with her conditioning. Eventually, the CEO became self-aware enough to shift her attitude. As she put it, "If I'm triggered, I'm being defensive. I'm not being creative." In future meetings she held her tongue when the director spoke and used her energy to get the board to focus on the important business at hand.

At other times, you can disarm a trigger by reaching out and asking for help from those on your team. At a very large bank in the United Kingdom, one of the executives we worked with got triggered by feeling disrespected at meetings. Sometimes he felt he was being talked over or that others were taking credit for his ideas. We suggested that he have a frank discussion with his team on why he felt this way—we asked him to be vulnerable. He told his team that he was triggered when he felt he wasn't being respected, and that he would shut down and not listen. When he said that, someone on the team said, "Okay, so what would get you out of it?" "Well," the executive replied, "I think, first, more openness. The fact that we can now tell each other what upsets us helps. Secondly, if you see me triggered, maybe it's because you did something that disrespected me." After the conversation, the team, now aware of the person's triggers, functioned more smoothly and the executive felt more engaged and energized. He had cleared the air.

So, what does vulnerability look like, and how can you maintain influence with your people if you at times reveal your own doubts and shortcomings? We have found that the more comfortable, open, truthful, and authentic you are, the more people open up to you and the more respect and valuable input you get from people. Remember, you're being vulnerable not just to share, but also to get input from others—it's about reaching out.

Reeta Roy, the CEO of the Mastercard Foundation, is someone who leads by example, is willing to be vulnerable, and believes in building relationships based on trust. Since 2008, she has headed one of the largest philanthropic organizations in the world, with about $40 billion in assets. By understanding who she is and having empathy for others, Roy has found the right balance between speaking the hard truth and being self-effacing. She is direct and has a clear vision for what needs to happen, but also the ability to deeply connect with people. She makes people feel valued and heard by genuinely asking for their opinions about how to approach challenges or solve problems.

In 2006, Mastercard created a foundation based in Toronto with the purpose of advancing education and financial inclusion. The board recruited Roy in 2008 to set a direction for this new charitable organization. She had been the divisional vice president of global citizenship and policy at the health care company Abbott. She enjoyed her job and working with her colleagues but was feeling restless and wondered if she was capable of more. It was time for a new challenge. In the early days of the Mastercard Foundation, she had no lack of advice from external parties. Focus on Canada, one suggested. Another said India was the logical choice, while still others indicated that with its extensive resources, the foundation could serve all corners of the world.

Roy eventually made what was, in the philanthropic world, a controversial choice. She informed the board that her vision for the foundation was to focus solely on sub-Saharan Africa. Some outside critics argued that Africa was corrupt and the money would not reach the right hands, while others said Africa did not have the capacity to absorb large amounts of funding. While Roy carefully considered others' perspectives and insights, she had clarity and believed in the opportunity even if others could not see it. Moreover, with a start-up foundation, Roy said, "I knew we had a real chance to have consequential impact in Africa."

Roy's strong conviction about Africa was based on what she had done her entire career—listen and learn from a diverse group of people. By doing so, she allowed herself to be vulnerable. She spent months traveling across Ethiopia, Kenya, Uganda, and Senegal, collecting data and insights and talking with community leaders, educators, entrepreneurs, and, most important, young people. She learned about barriers that women faced in accessing finance for their businesses or to educate their children. She heard about constraints on institutions and nongovernmental organizations that wanted to offer services to those living in poverty. "To build a vision and strategy," she recalls, "you have to ask a few simple questions and humble yourself to learn. Otherwise, you miss out on insights. Even though I had traveled a lot and worked in East Africa, I was naïve about Africa."

She concluded that the continent posed a once-in-a-lifetime opportunity. For one thing, the workforce was young—the majority were under the age of thirty and eager for change. Roy thought that if they had greater access to education, better financial tools and networks, they would be able to fully participate in the economy. And this in turn would have a multiplier effect on generating prosperity.

When she returned to Canada and shared her new vision with the board, they signed off without reservation. In the following years, the foundation built programs with many partners across Africa. This enabled young people, especially young women, to secure their education and supported micro-entrepreneurs with access to finance and markets. By the end of 2016, approximately twenty million people had accessed financial services through these programs.

After a decade of work, Roy, her board, and her colleagues paused to review their learnings and achievements, as well as assess any missed opportunities. They asked young people, leaders, and communities about where the foundation should concentrate its efforts over the next decade. This led to the launch of Young Africa Works in 2018—a strategy to address youth unemployment in Africa. To execute the strategy, Roy and her team quickly realized that they would also need to transform their organization and establish a presence in Africa. So in 2019, Roy moved to Kigali, Rwanda. Today, most of the foundation's staff and leaders are African and are based in seven countries. Despite the disruption caused by the COVID-19 pandemic, by the end of 2023, 65 percent of the foundation's partners were African organizations, it had helped 6.6 million young people find work, and millions more had accessed skills training and financial services through the foundation's programs.

Roy's road to success, however, wasn't easy. She grew up in Malaysia. After her father passed away when she was only fourteen, her family was left with little money. Roy learned humility and courage from her mother, who was determined to educate her daughter and son. Roy says, "My first scholarship was my mother's scholarship." Her mother mortgaged her only asset, her house, to enable Roy to attend high school in North Carolina. "My mother told me, 'I can get you there, but after that, you'll need to find your way.'" Roy won a scholarship to attend St. Andrews Presbyterian College (now St. Andrews University). To earn pocket money, she took various jobs working in the cafeteria, as an aide to a disabled student, and providing administrative support to a professor. "The first value for me," she says, "has always been about humility, and that comes from my childhood. Any organization or any individual who has great wealth or great power needs to be self-aware and big enough to recognize that there's so much they don't know and need to learn. Think of it as enlightened self-interest."

She continues, "Too many of us seek to balance competing demands by compartmentalizing our lives into tidy personal and professional segments. Yet we inhabit multiple spheres, and our lives are more often messy than orderly. Balance is better measured not by time allocated on a calendar, but by experiences over a lifetime. Leadership is about living, empathizing, learning, and giving of ourselves."

In the years she spent building the Mastercard Foundation, this perspective helped her to make the right decisions during some difficult situations. For Roy, this meant treating people with respect. When the foundation, for example, collected data and insights about economic conditions or problems facing villages, marketplaces, farming communities, or schools, they didn't assume that they owned all the data. They would return to the people who were their sources to discuss what they learned and to ask for their input and ideas to create solutions. "We would share what we heard from them," says Roy, "and ask, 'Does it resonate with you?' When you don't listen, you can potentially make the wrong decision and miss an opportunity to make a real difference."

For example, in the foundation's early days, a nongovernmental organization proposed a microfinancing program, which offered very low-interest loans to aspiring young African entrepreneurs. Six months into the program, not a single loan had been issued. Roy and her team visited the country and discovered that these young people did not want loans. They wanted savings accounts. So they pivoted and changed the program. It was an example of how preconceived assumptions had gotten in the way of providing the community with what it really needed. This kind of openness and willingness to admit mistakes led to a stronger working relationship with the community.

Sometimes being vulnerable means having to put aside one's pride and apologize. While the foundation was developing its youth employment strategy, it sent staff to an African country on a fact-finding mission. Unfortunately, the staffers did not appreciate the cultural norms in the country and did not ask for guidance from others who did. Thus they missed certain cues in discussions with government officials and made some poor judgment calls. Roy got word that they had offended the government. After seeking advice, she requested a meeting with the country's president. She explained the foundation's strategy and apologized for the misstep. As their discussion concluded, the president told

Roy, "I consider today the first day of our partnership." For Roy, it was a gracious expression of trust.

On another occasion, Roy participated in a meeting with a partner organization to discuss the progress of a program and how it could be expanded. About twenty staff members from the foundation and the organization were sitting in an intimate circle. Things seemed to be going well, until the leader of the partner organization abruptly interrupted the conversation and stated, "The foundation has not treated us right. You make us feel like we have to beg for money, and that's not right." After some further discussion, they learned that someone at the foundation had been unresponsive to their inquiries regarding when they could begin the program. Without hesitation, Roy stood and apologized. "I said, 'Thank you for being candid. You should expect better from us, and we will take action to change.' And we did."

Roy used these situations as learning experiences for the foundation and a way to engage her colleagues on how things can go wrong and how they can be turned around. The dialogue also serves as a reminder that the values of the foundation always need to be visible in individual actions and behaviors. "These are watershed moments. Periodically, we need to remind ourselves that to achieve significant impact, we need to develop trust-based and productive working relationships with our partners."

Another attitude that Roy embraces—and which is closely aligned to being vulnerable—is not to take oneself too seriously. It's difficult to open yourself up to others and to really understand people if you spend your time worrying about yourself and your own status and prestige. A little perspective and some humor never hurt. When problems seem insurmountable, it helps to step back and put things in perspective. According to Roy, "That's when you see what's truly important. Ask yourself,

'Am I doing my best?' In terms of the age of the planet, our life is a nanosecond. So, what will you do with your nanosecond?"

Allowing yourself to be vulnerable does entail a risk. It can, if not handled properly, diminish your influence in the eyes of some. In a world where hierarchies are fluid and leaders project humility and vulnerability, how do you balance that with the need to command respect? If you dress the same as the rank and file and work in an open office layout surrounded by others, it's easy for you to seem vulnerable and you can start losing influence. You have to establish your presence as the leader. "That's a tough balancing act to pull off," says former Novartis CEO Dan Vasella. "Leaders now gain respect by being both competent and honest. That doesn't mean that you say everything you think, but you have to be authentic. If you have that and you know what you're doing, people will see that you are in charge."

Being in charge means having the strength to set the direction of the organization without being led in different directions by your followers. You must understand the context of the situation and gather the views of others, but in the end it's the leader's job to make the hard decisions. "As a leader," says Vasella, "your job is to recognize the right goal and path forward and then to align and persuade people to do the things you believe will be relevant for the long-term success of the company. People want you to lead. And if you lead, you will also hurt. You will satisfy sometimes. You will celebrate and you will provide tough feedback in a human way. That's all part of your job. You must have the backbone and the integrity to be straight with people."

As we've discussed, being transparent is essential to being an inspirational leader. But that transparency comes with a cost. Because your reports feel more comfortable confronting you and your ideas, you can feel more vulnerable—and not in a good way. A lot is being projected on you, as if you were a movie screen onto which people put all their positive and negative past experiences with authority. It can be tough to take all that scrutiny day after day. Having personally been in that position throughout his career, Vasella has a helpful take on the topic. "You have to understand that all the criticism is not necessarily about you. It's what you represent for them. It's the institution or a past authority they're taking aim at, not you as the person you are. The CEO is the office, not an individual." In our conversations at the Bower Forum, some of the participants said that when the heat was turned up on them, they started to take the criticism personally and began to think that maybe they weren't the right person for the job. "You have to ignore the reality distortion field to be a good leader," says Vasella, "and that applies to all levels, to any boss. It's mostly about the office, not you. It's the only way to stay sane."

Most—if not all—leaders have a to-do list that keeps them on track. But how many have a "to-be" list—a reminder of who you are and how you want to behave when you show up at work every day? Are you egotistical or open to others? Are you snappish or warm? Are you emotionally distant or vulnerable? Essentially, the to-be list is anchored in the human characteristics of your leadership style, and is also linked to the core traits of your character.

Balancing being strong and being vulnerable isn't easy. When you're the top dog, people expect you to be strong, certain, and determined. There's a time for that, however, and a time to be vulnerable. Leaders, for example, have to make tough decisions on firing, budget allocation, promotions, and pay—you can't give up your decision-making power. But you should open yourself to others to get analytical and emotional feedback—ideally from people with multiple perspectives—*before* making those tough decisions.

When he was running Cincinnati Children's Hospital Medical Center, Michael Fisher maintained that fine balance between having influence and showing his vulnerability. In the spring of 2020, after the murder of George Floyd, a Black man who was killed by a Minneapolis police officer during his arrest, demonstrations erupted throughout the United States. At that time, Fisher, who had worked hard on diversity, equity, and inclusion issues for years, held some listening sessions with a number of his Black employees to see how he and the institution could better support them. "I remember crying on more than one occasion as I heard some of the experiences our Black employees had in our workplace," says Fisher. "Some of what I heard really hurt and touched me, and I think showing that vulnerability helped me develop a deeper connection with employees and better insights on the actions we needed to take as an organization."

In 2018, when Fisher was diagnosed with cancer and had to take a six-month leave, he struggled with how to share the news. He was a private person, and his instinct was to quietly go away and get treatment. He felt, however, that it was important for the employees and other stakeholders at Cincinnati Children's to know what was going on. So he created a series of communications. First was a letter to all employees and the community announcing that he was sick and explaining how long he thought he'd be gone. Next, he created two videos. In the first, he gave a progress report while he was in the middle of intense chemotherapy. In the second, he announced that he was in remission and would return to his job in a few weeks. "It's tough to balance being vulnerable with keeping your influence," says Fisher, "but we're human beings, and people want to work with real people who are transparent, authentic, and who role model the behaviors and values of the team and institution."

Questions to ask yourself about vulnerability:

- Do I have the courage to put myself out there, willing to take the chance of failing and showing my vulnerabilities?

- Am I seen as I truly am or as the executive in a given role? How can I change my behavior so that I'm seen as the person I am?

- Do I share my greatest strengths, hopes, dreams, concerns, anxieties, and questions—even if I fear being judged?

- Am I snappish or warm? Emotionally distant or authentic?

- What holds me back from showing my emotional characteristics more? What will help me embrace the courage that comes with vulnerability rather than fear the weakness it may expose?

- All leaders have a to-do list. Do I have a to-be list—a reminder of who I am and how I want to behave when I show up at work every day?

- What is my current to-be list? Who can be a thought partner to develop my future to-be list?

In Summary

///

Being vulnerable means you are in touch with what triggers your emotions and know how to direct those feelings into positive energy. You are willing to be touched, moved, and influenced by others and at the same time to share your hopes, fears, and concerns in a way that invites support from others. It is a sign of strength rather than weakness. As University of Houston professor and author Brené Brown puts it, "Vulnerability is Power."

Going through vulnerable experiences is an untapped source of growth and development for many executives, as we have learned at many Bower Forum sessions over the years. It is essential to be vulnerable in the right situations and to practice leading from the inside out. The art lies in being thoughtful about when, where, and how to be vulnerable. Yet life does not always go as planned. Being vulnerable also means knowing how to deal with failure.

5

SO YOU FAILED. NOW WHAT?

A t a McKinsey leadership event held in London, thirty women executives from diverse industries and around the globe were asked to write a story about a situation where something went wrong and they felt like a failure. When the women started to share their stories with the group, the first was in tears by the end of her presentation. Then the second woman began, and by the time she finished she was clearly very upset. What quickly became apparent was that even within this high-powered group of women—after all, their companies wouldn't have sent them to this international event if they didn't believe they had tremendous potential—everyone had a story about a failure. "What I realized," said one woman attending the event, "is that what matters is not whether you at times fail—because everyone does—but how you deal with it. The people who succeed are the ones who know how not to get caught in a downward spiral, who focus their energies on moving forward and getting out of it. And that's the secret sauce."

When failure hits, most people don't want to talk about it—which is only natural. Yet failure is becoming more common as the world becomes more complex and change comes at a faster and faster pace—to the extent that it's hard to imagine anyone who won't fail at least once or twice throughout a career. Traditionally, you earned a degree, built a career for forty or so years, and then retired by sixty-five. That paradigm is shifting. One way to think about it is that life spans are increasing, and soon it won't be unusual for people to work for fifty or sixty years or longer. In a sense, you need to design for a hundred-year life. Over that time span, you are more likely to lose your job or feel stuck simply because you'll be working longer. The point is, if you dare to do great things, if you put yourself out there and go for the big prize, you will sometimes fail.

When you fail, you experience one or more of an array of emotions—guilt, anger, insecurity, self-pity. Many feel that they've failed the company and their colleagues. Others bury their pain. The fifth element of our leadership process is resilience. Executives in these sessions learn that those who bounce back fastest don't waste a lot of time asking why something bad happened to them. Instead, they focus their time and energy on understanding whether it was some behavior, bias, or blind spot that was at the root of their failure, and then they adjust accordingly. They learn that the best way to bounce forward is to pause briefly and make sure they carry forward any lesson learned from the mishap.

The business world has no lack of resilient leaders. Early in his career, Walt Disney was fired from an ad agency for a "singular lack of drawing ability." Disney and Henry Ford both went bankrupt with early ventures, and Steve Jobs got a pink slip from Apple. He spent years in exile before returning to create what became one of the greatest tech companies in history. As a young executive at General Electric, Jack Welch, who would eventually become CEO, once blew up a pilot plastics plant and was blamed for its faulty design. In one of its most celebrated cover stories, "So You Fail. Now Bounce Back!," *Fortune* magazine told the story of how Coca-Cola CEO Roberto Goizueta appointed Sergio Zyman, the risk-loving leader who launched New Coke, the biggest corporate failure since the Edsel, to be his new head of global marketing. As Goizueta explained to *Fortune*, "We became uncompetitive by not being tolerant of mistakes. The moment you let avoiding failure become your motivator, you're down the path of inactivity. You can stumble only if you're moving."

Sometimes we see executives who have become their own worst enemies. Their emotions get the best of them, and instead of looking ahead and being optimistic about their prospects, they wallow in their disappointment. As we discussed in chapter 4, the best leaders understand what is triggering their anger and fear. Finding where their personal turmoil comes from—whether it's justified or not—helps them confront their anger in order to put it behind them. This is particularly hard for individuals when their anger feels justified. At one Bower Forum, a talented executive who rose to the C-suite of a Fortune 100 global consumer products company was passed over for the CEO job, and this failure made him furious. Even though he was only in his mid-forties, he believed he had the talent to do the job, but now he felt slighted and was stewing over the idea that a particular board member had sabotaged his bid.

After taking a deep dive on his situation, the executive realized that if he was going to progress in his career, he had to put his anger behind him and learn to develop more stamina and resistance. The way to do that, one of the more seasoned leaders told him, was to "learn to appreciate your capabilities, and to reflect upon not only what you have already accomplished, but what you could accomplish. Because if you stay bitter and negative for a long time it will further derail your career." Taking their advice, the executive started to reach outside his company to make more contacts and raise his profile. He was eventually hired as the CEO of a large European health products company where he was a resounding success.

Fear of failure always leads to some form of ego fear. Ask yourself, "What would be the very worst if I failed? What would this say about me? What feels at stake?" Typically, the answer will be you're not loved, not achieving, you're letting others down, or not being good enough. The fear of failure can lead us to play not to lose. However, if we reframe failure as the love of learning in the service of a bigger vision, we start to take more personal risks in service of something bigger than ourselves. We start to play to win. Are you solving for avoiding failures or for learning faster in service of something bigger than yourself?

The best CEOs learn how to approach everyday failures, no matter how seemingly minor, as learning experiences. When you embrace your fear of failure, you can discover what needs to change and then create experiments to test, learn, and adapt. The idea is to focus on harvesting valuable lessons from your missteps, because to avoid failure is to avoid learning, and that can be costly in an increasingly complex and unpredictable world. Successful leaders calmly analyze the root cause of a situation, adjust their behavior, and then bounce forward.

One CEO of a global tech company had had a bumpy career. He had been fired years back from his company for being arrogant, took another CEO job, but then returned later to his old company as CEO, having learned from his past failures. At one point the CEO was addressing his top 150 executives at an event and was doing a good job of inspiring his troops. Then, while recognizing and praising his new chief human resources officer (CHRO), he said that the company had never had a great CHRO. The woman who had done the job before was sitting right beside her replacement. Then a woman in the audience asked him a question about diversity, equity, and inclusion (DEI), and he dismissed it unintentionally. After the meeting he was talking with one of his trusted advisers, who told him that his words at the event had turned off a lot of people. He hadn't realized his impact, but after thinking about it, he knew he had to rectify the situation. The next day he shifted his calendar so he could return to the event. He brought with him the woman who used to be the CHRO and made a public apology to her and praised her willingness to take the job in a tough time until they could hire another CHRO. He then in front of the entire group apologized to the woman who had asked the DEI question and recognized her for her courage to always speak the truth. He had made two bad mistakes, but in the end had bounced forward, turning the negative impact he had made on his people into a positive experience for himself and his organization. True strength of character gets built by admitting mistakes and turning them into lessons.

People can fail because of circumstances or bad luck or making the wrong decision. But in some situations, leaders might do well to take a hard look at themselves. Perhaps it's the way they think and behave that's really keeping them back either from the next promotion or, in the case of a CEO, from reaching that next level of performance. That's when it's time to reinvent yourself.

One of our favorite reinvention stories of an executive bouncing forward from a setback is that of Claire Babineaux-Fontenot, the CEO of the nonprofit Feeding America. Under her guidance, Feeding America has become the nation's largest domestic hunger relief organization and largest U.S. charity, according to *Forbes*. Babineaux-Fontenot oversees a network of more than two hundred food banks, twenty-one statewide food bank associations, and sixty thousand partner agencies, food pantries, and meal programs. In fiscal year 2021, Feeding America provided 6.6 *billion* meals to tens of millions of people in need. Babineaux-Fontenot, however, wasn't always riding this high.

Born in rural Louisiana, Babineaux-Fontenot grew up in a large working-class family—her parents were both children of sharecroppers. From age twelve, she knew she wanted to become a lawyer, and the lessons that her parents taught her about self-reliance and self-sacrifice served her well. She heard stories about how her mother sacrificed her own education to stay at home and work so her siblings could attend school. Her parents stressed (and expected) that anyone in her family—including siblings with developmental and behavioral obstacles—could, if they put their mind to it, succeed in life. "The most impactful education that I received," she says, "was not in the classroom but at home where I learned to take responsibility for my own success. Later in life that helped me realize what it meant to show up at work as an adult and then show up at home as a mom and a wife and a daughter and a sister who's an adult."

After she graduated from law school, Babineaux-Fontenot's career began to take off. She earned her master of laws in taxation, then worked as the assistant secretary of the Office of Legal Affairs for the state of Louisiana's revenue department, then in big four accounting at the consulting and audit firm PwC, and then at the law firm of Adams and Reese, where she led its tax practice and was the partner in charge of its Baton Rouge office. Walmart, one of her clients at both PwC and Adams and Reese, noticed her and asked her to join their tax department in 2004.

At first the job seemed like a dream to Babineaux-Fontenot, the culmination of everything she had been working so hard to achieve. Walmart had created a new role for her—VP of audits and tax policy. Between the time she accepted the new role and when she arrived to start work, the size of her team doubled and then doubled again every four months or so. Babineaux-Fontenot started to feel in over her head. "Every other role I ever had," she says, "was one where somebody said, 'Oh, she's doing a good job at that; let's just take her next assignment up one hair.' Suddenly Walmart was asking me to take this huge leap."

After two years on the job, her boss asked her if she'd like to be the corporation's chief tax officer. When she accepted, her boss asked her how long she needed to prepare for the job. Figuring that she had to keep doing her current job while figuring out how to run Walmart's global tax department, she said she needed twelve months. Two weeks later they announced that she was starting the job immediately. She said to herself, "Oh my God, what do they think they're doing?"

At that point Babineaux-Fontenot says she fell "hard and heavy" into impostor syndrome. "I was so insecure in my ability to deliver, I thought they got it wrong. It was a terrible idea. I wasn't ready. But I didn't want to fail at being the first African American woman to be the chief tax officer at the Fortune 500's biggest company. I felt compelled to plow ahead." In the early days as chief tax officer, Babineaux-Fontenot felt out of her league and looked for a corporate model to follow. The only one she could find was the previous tax chief. He was the person who had hired her at Walmart and had been one of her clients when she was at the law firm. So she started doing what he did, trying to be like him. But things weren't going well. She tried to act like she had all the answers, but she was overwhelmed, was falling behind, and felt like a failure for the first time in her career. "I don't do well being a middle-aged white man from Alabama," says Babineaux-Fontenot. "I played the role badly and saw myself failing miserably, and the problem with failure is that you never fail by yourself. I was dragging down my department."

After going through some tough self-assessment, she realized that something had to change. In her annual evaluation, she told her boss that what she was doing wasn't working. "I told him that if I were going to fail, I was going to fail while being me, not an imitation of somebody else." Her boss said she was being too hard on herself. And she told him that "his expectations were too low." Then Babineaux-Fontenot informed him she was going to set a new bar for her department in tax efficiency. He chuckled, shook his head, and said that no one at the company had ever achieved that level of tax savings.

Walking away from her boss's office, Babineaux-Fontenot thought to herself, "How on earth am I going to do what I just signed up for?" She shared her idea with her team, and they were flabbergasted. The stretch goal was too much. At one point she was driving from Walmart's headquarters to Little Rock with a member of her executive team, and he said to her, "Claire, I don't know if you are really thinking about what you're doing here, but you're setting these expectations, and the brass are going to expect us to do this, and if we don't, there will be repercussions."

For the first time in her career, Babineaux-Fontenot was being asked to do something beyond her personal expertise. She had worked in highly technical tax and tax litigation roles, but nothing prepared her to run such a large and complicated organization. She said to herself, "I know how to build a team and I know in my bones that diverse and inclusive teams win." So she built a team that filled in her gaps in knowledge and leadership experience, and asked everyone to work to their highest capacity. She displayed the kind of humility that allowed her to admit she didn't have everything it takes to do such a big job and hired people who would bring diverse ideas and challenge her. She relied on her ability to spot great talent, and it worked. Ultimately, as Walmart's chief tax officer, Babineaux-Fontenot surpassed that tax efficiency stretch goal she had promised her boss.

———

Failure, however, isn't just about not performing well. Sometimes someone fails through no fault of their own: The world has changed, markets have dried up, or new technologies have emerged. Perhaps the kind of job that you were doing is no longer needed, or the organization is downsizing. We've found that failure can also be very personal. Some leaders talked about how they stopped learning in their jobs and felt stuck. Others said they felt like they'd been doing the same job or working in the same industry for too long. Others still simply said they felt burned out. In other words, they felt like they'd failed.

Anju Patwardhan, working at Citibank in Singapore in the mid-2000s, felt it was time for a change. She could boast of a successful fifteen-year career working up the corporate ladder. A skilled risk manager, Patwardhan was doing well in her job but felt she needed a fresh challenge, something that would challenge her intellectually. But where to turn? What was that job and who could help her find it? A colleague suggested that she draw a chart of her networks, including her internal and external circles, her mentors, and her sages. When she did, she discovered that she had a very limited network outside the bank. For most of her career she had internally focused jobs. She was in operations, then in audit, digital banking, and risk management, with a focus on fintech. While people in the bank knew her well, she had what she calls a "zero external profile." She needed to reach out to someone who could help her find a new career. Patwardhan began the hard work of building circles of influence outside her company. She attended events and leadership training programs and accepted as many speaking engagements as she could. Eventually she built a rich external network.

Thanks to her networking efforts, she was invited to speak on a panel on fintech at the World Economic Forum. There she struck up a conversation with one of the panelists, Tang Ning, an entrepreneur who ran a large company in China that had several business lines including a fintech VC fund called CreditEase. The two got along, but Patwardhan thought nothing of it at the time.

When she turned forty, she gathered her courage and left her job at Citibank. "I thought I was going to retire," recalls Patwardhan. "I had never taken a break. I had gone straight from school to engineering to MBA to job. And you know, I used to feel jealous of people who took breaks in between. And I said, 'Okay, let me try retirement.'" Relying on her new network, she became a certified docent and got a job at the Singapore Art Museum. She trained to become a volunteer at a woman's helpline. She and her husband traveled around the world, but she did not find her new life satisfying. Patwardhan failed at retirement, but she learned something important about herself. She realized that she could not go from working full time in a demanding corporate role to volunteer work. She missed the intellectual stimulation of her previous role, and she missed being with like-minded people. She knew she had to go back to work. She enjoyed it too much.

So, a few months after she left Citibank, she took a job at Standard Chartered bank, working in various roles over the years, including as chief operating officer, chief risk officer, and global chief innovation officer. Her job required her to stay on top of all the emerging fintech companies and see which would make a good fit for the bank. She was enjoying her work, but as time passed, she realized that she was still stuck in traditional banking and felt restless. Her job at Standard Chartered often brought her to Silicon Valley as she managed the bank's innovation lab there, and she fell in love with the Bay Area and its energy. She started thinking about how she could live there. "I wasn't sure what I wanted to do," says Patwardhan, "but I knew that I didn't want to go to another bank because I already had the best possible job in banking. I also knew that I had limited runway in the bank, and I wanted to figure out what I wanted to do next before I got pushed out—which is what eventually happens to everyone."

With a lust for learning in her DNA, Patwardhan considered leaving Standard Chartered and getting a PhD, but that seemed like a lot of hard work. In 2015 she was speaking at a fintech panel at Stanford University—a result of her decision to build out her external networks—and discovered that one of the people on the panel was a Fulbright Visiting Scholar. She asked him more about the program. It was the same program one of Patwardhan's idols, Madeleine Albright, had attended. Albright started her career late in life at age forty and built an amazingly varied career over the next four decades that included being a member of the U.S. National Security Council, a professor at Georgetown, a secretary of state, and the head of a political consulting firm that bore her name. "Suddenly," said Patwardhan, "all these light bulbs started flashing. I could change my career." She applied, was accepted, and began getting ready to move to Palo Alto to start her research at Stanford on how to use technology for financial inclusion.

As she was getting ready to leave for California, Tang Ning, the entrepreneur she had met earlier on that panel at the World Economic Forum, visited Singapore and invited her to breakfast at a restaurant in the city's financial district. They had three meetings that week, and he asked her to run his fintech VC fund, which was based in the Bay Area. Patwardhan was nervous at first. She had always worked at a large global bank, and heading a VC fund was something she had never done. She was not one to shy away from new challenges and had often asked for new, demanding roles in Citibank and in Standard Chartered, but this felt like a bridge too far, in a new industry and on a new continent. Ning felt that Patwardhan should join the fund even though she told him she didn't know anything about investing. His logic was that the fund had former investment bankers and analysts who knew a lot about valuations, but it needed someone with a strong operating background.

His persuasive powers proved too much, and after she arrived in California, she started advising the fund on a part-time basis. About her networking experience, Patwardhan likes to joke, "I always tell people the moral of the story is, don't be a keynote speaker. Be on panels. That's how I found out about the Fulbright program and ended up in a VC fund. Being a keynote speaker is hard work. It requires a lot of preparation, and you don't get to meet all these interesting people who might change the trajectory of your career."

When she arrived in California, she knew she didn't have all the skills needed to make venture investments at the fintech VC fund. So she signed up for six courses in her first semester at Stanford on topics that included venture capital investing, private equity investing, emerging markets investing, and how to build tech start-ups. Through her courses she met venture capitalists, entrepreneurs, and professors whom she added to her ever-growing network. "I was now part of this billion-dollar fund which was making investments, and everything was happening very fast. I was in the classroom. I was trying to figure out what our strategy should be—what works and what doesn't work and what you can do as a Chinese fund and what you cannot do in the U.S. It was an accelerated learning process. I got to sit opposite some of the smartest people in the world who shared what they're doing and why."

About a year after she started advising the fintech fund, Patwardhan started running it. As of 2022, CE Innovation Capital had invested in over a hundred companies globally. She invested in over forty-five companies—twenty of which became unicorns, which means they were valued at $1 billion or more. Most recently, Patwardhan has moved back to Singapore, but she still helps manage many of the fund's original investments. While she was at Stanford, she collaborated with Professor Ken Singleton at the business school to launch a fintech course for MBA students and continued to be a guest speaker for the course. She recently did her Bellagio Residency in Italy through the Rockefeller Foundation, where she focused on longevity and financial well-being. Her current passion is to help older adults think about their personal finances in an age where more and more of them will live to be a hundred years old. Most recently, she helped create a course called "Designing for the 100-Year Life," which is taught at the National University of Singapore.

From global banker to Fulbright Scholar to a fintech VC fund manager to a teacher and researcher, Patwardhan displayed the kind of resilience in her life that allowed her to reinvent herself whenever she felt blocked or dissatisfied with what she was doing. She could do this because she was curious, had built a strong network of contacts, and had the courage to try something new. "If I remain in the same role for three years or more," she says, "I start feeling like I'm not being challenged enough, I'm not learning anything new, so I need to move on. To do this you must acknowledge that you're not the smartest person in the room. If you want to do something new, you sometimes need to ask questions that can make you look stupid. And I excel at that. I have no problem saying that I don't know, so please help me understand." Patwardhan is always willing to pursue a new path in life, whenever she feels, by her own definition, that she is getting stuck. In large part, it explains why her own path has been so successful.

Another topic that often came up at the Bower Forum was using passion to overcome a feeling of failure. The challenge is to find a job or profession that doesn't feel like work. Look for jobs where you can learn and grow. And be sure you're working for more than the money. "One of the big takeaways for me after living in Silicon Valley," says Patwardhan, "was that it's not all about making money. It's about doing things that give you joy. You have to identify what gives you joy. And for me, what gives me joy is being surrounded by people who are intellectually very smart, and I can learn something from them, and they can learn something from me. So I'm always thinking about how to create more opportunities like that."

When you fail, it's important to have a method to bring yourself out of your negative thoughts and overcome a feeling of failure. Often, we get caught up in a simple story about ourselves. We say to ourselves, "I didn't really fail; it's someone else's fault," or "I was right, but outside forces caused me to fail." But this isn't addressing the true reason for failure and will leave a lingering feeling of unease deep inside you. Asking the question "How might I be wrong?" can help us gain one or more new perspectives on what actually happened. By doing this, we discover new stories about ourselves, which help us bounce forward from failure. In this technique, you take the situation—what actually happened to make you feel that you've failed—and look at it from a different perspective. You might have been too proud to listen to the advice of a valued colleague. Or, being too wedded to your own opinions, you might have ignored market signals that called for a change in course. The point is to hit the pause button and give yourself time to discover the real reason for your failure so you can acknowledge it, figure out how you need to change, and then move on.

Questions to ask yourself about the fear of failure and how to turn failure into personal growth:

//

- What are the root causes driving my fear of failure? How can I address them?

- Am I afraid to take risks for fear of letting others down?

- What would be the very worst thing to happen if I failed? What would this say about me? What feels at stake?

- Am I playing "not to lose" out of a fear of failure? What do I stand to gain if I dare to try?

- How can I build the muscle to declare when it is time to cut losses and benefit from what I learned?

- How can I reframe failure as the love of learning in the service of a bigger vision for myself and my teams? How can I use it to spur growth and development?

- How can I learn to take more personal risks in the service of something bigger than myself?

//

In Summary

//

Leaders who manage failure well are honest with themselves about their own shortcomings and have both the resilience to bounce forward from a bad situation and the ability to apply the lessons learned going forward. As the professional poker player Annie Duke argues, you have to balance "quit and grit," which means knowing when to persevere in a bad situation and when to cut your losses. This requires deep inner reflection over when and when not to take certain risks in light of the potential gains, and how to learn from failures—another dimension for a leader to learn to lead from the inside out.

This highlights another important characteristic of great leaders: versatility. The best develop multiple skills and engage in deep learning and therefore are able to adapt swiftly in the face of uncertainty or constant crisis—versatility not only around the emotional but also the intellectual aspects of leadership.

6

Versatility

LEARN TO BE AGILE

he CEOs who come to the Bower Forum typically dwell on a single thorny problem that keeps them awake at night. At this session, however, a seasoned CEO told her group that she was getting hit from all sides. She had risen through the ranks by growing one area of her media conglomerate, but now she needed to cut costs at a money-losing division and didn't feel she had the right skills to get the job done. She was also trying to master the intricacies of video streaming but was struggling to understand how to gain a competitive advantage. Worse still, she had gotten herself into a spat over LGBTQ issues, and some right-wing politicians accused her of running a "woke" corporation. "I might be able to handle one of these challenges," she complained, "but how do I juggle all three at once?"

This CEO is not alone. Today's leaders must cope with a growing and shifting number of challenging externalities, from supply-chain disruptions to inflation to political polarization to global unrest—all while running their organization. That's a tall task by any measure. And these just happen to be today's challenges. In the next few years, it is all but certain that an entirely new set of external challenges will test the resolve and skills of every leader. At the same time, an ever-expanding lineup of constituents—investors, activists, employees, government officials, the media—are pressuring CEOs, who in the end need their approval in order to succeed.

As we've seen in the previous five chapters of this book, dealing with all these challenges requires balancing a mix of humility, confidence, selflessness, vulnerability, and resilience. Leaders will soon find, however, that these qualities, while crucial, are not sufficient to get the job done. In the sixth and final leadership element of part 1, we coach leaders to add another weapon to their arsenal. They need to learn to be versatile. As we will explore in this chapter, the best leaders are versatile in the following three ways: They have pursued diverse experiences in their careers, they are constantly curious to learn new things, and they have mastered the dynamics of interacting with varied groups of stakeholders.

Some of the most innovative and creative people in history succeeded because they were versatile—able to master more than one discipline and often benefiting from blending the knowledge of those varied subject matters to come up with new ideas and inventions. Benjamin Franklin was a skilled writer and printer, and a renowned scientist who made significant contributions, including the invention of the lightning rod and bifocal glasses. In the political field, he played a key role in drafting the Declaration of Independence and negotiating the Treaty of Paris to end the American Revolution. Franklin's experience in the printing industry and his interest in literature led him to create *Poor Richard's Almanack*, a yearly publication that contained a mix of practical advice, weather predictions, and philosophical musings. By drawing on different fields, Franklin created a publication that was both informative and entertaining, and that helped to shape American political thought.

What does versatility mean in the business world? Leaders need to master two types of versatility: internal versatility and the versatility of experiences gained from interacting within an organization and dealing with outside stakeholders. We've already explored the ins and outs of internal versatility in part 1 of this book. We saw examples of leaders who broadened their range by being able to be both humble and bold, both vulnerable and strong, and who could embrace failure but bounced forward. This chapter, however, is about managing the versatility of experience. It's about knowing how to go broad, when to go deep, and how and when to expand your range by seeking others who can help expose you to diverse types of experience. It's about being good at what you do but also knowing how to get out of your comfort zone by challenging yourself and your organization, by constantly asking questions and being curious.

DO WHAT MAKES YOU UNCOMFORTABLE

One thing we noticed about successful leaders is that most would credit their career trajectory to a singular formula. Some make it to the top by being marketing whizzes. Others are skillful cost cutters and restructurers. Others still earn their reputation by knowing how to grow a business. Whatever the bundle of skills, the truth is that most of us operate in only one basic mode. We do what we're good at and get rewarded for that behavior. Chances are you got promoted to a new position because your boss needed a savvy cost cutter or someone who could grow a new venture into a powerhouse. You were the obvious choice.

The trouble with having a single strength is that it might not always be what's needed to run a large, complicated organization. John Plant, the CEO of Howmet Aerospace and a Bower Forum coach, says, "So you get hired as CEO and you manage well the first phase of the cycle, which might require someone who has restructuring skills. But then the company, after three or four years, pivots to a growth mode, and because you don't have the right skills, the board may fire you. Very few people have the experience or versatility to be able to operate in those different modes."

In 2000, for example, when the dot-com stock bubble burst, the leaders of those online companies, who had been nurturing fast growth for years, suddenly found themselves managing for profitability. Instead of spending whatever it might take to grow, they now had to pivot and find ways to save money by laying people off, canceling projects, and finding waste. Many companies, like pets.com, Webvan, and boo.com, didn't survive. Those are two entirely different sets of muscles, and a leader has to be versatile to make the switch. Much of this comes down to what kind of experience the leader has. If you lack certain types of experience, the key is to find the right people both inside and outside the organization to complement your gaps.

Those striving to become CEOs should make sure that during their career they are putting themselves into varied environments, situations, and challenges where they can grow a varied set of skills. At one point they might volunteer to, say, help with a big restructuring. At another point, they might decide to go and run a midsize company that wants to grow from $500 million in revenue to $5 billion over the next five years. So when building your career, ask the question the right way. It's not how you become a versatile CEO but how you prepare yourself to become a versatile CEO. Says former Ford CEO Mark Fields, "Just because I say I want to be ten pounds lighter and three inches taller doesn't mean it's going to happen. But if you're putting yourself in positions in your career to get these different experiences, you're going to learn how to be a utility infielder and you will have that muscle memory that you'll need when you have to pivot from growth to cost cutting."

As we've noted, if you end up being CEO and you didn't have a chance to develop a full toolbox of skills and experiences on your way up, look for others around you who can speed up your learning curve. Michael Fisher, who has been CEO of three organizations—the nonprofit Cincinnati Children's Hospital Medical Center, the global automotive supplier company Premier Manufacturing Support Services, and the Cincinnati USA Regional Chamber of Commerce—says that on his way up the ladder he found that people in each of these spheres genuinely wanted to share their knowledge and be helpful. Early in his career, soon after he graduated from Stanford, he was an associate athletic director at Northwestern University, managing all their sports except for football and men's basketball. "I was aware," he says, "that I was never going to know more about women's field hockey or men's baseball than those coaches did, so I spent time building my relationships with them and understanding how I could help them to be successful."

Fisher kept that mindset throughout his career. When he was running Premier Manufacturing Support Services, he hired a former General Motors maintenance superintendent with deep experience who had worked all over the world, and peppered him with questions until he felt comfortable in an industry that was new to him. At Cincinnati Children's, Fisher learned that versatility also meant knowing when to take the lead and when not to. When COVID struck, the hospital switched into high gear to protect its staff and patients. Fisher could have led that effort himself, but it would have taken precious time from his other duties, including maintaining employee morale, strengthening trust, and protecting long-term institutional performance and viability. Instead, he allowed others to take the lead, in this case his chief operating officer, who was on point for managing the day-to-day pandemic protocols.

Another thing that Fisher says helped him to become more versatile was joining a number of nonprofit boards, including the United Way, where he got to watch a lot of good leaders operate, such as C-suite executives from Procter & Gamble, General Electric, Kroger, and Fifth Third Bank. "I often encourage younger leaders to serve on a not-for-profit board and get involved. You will have an opportunity to learn something new. You can start to hone your skills by understanding the nonprofit's strategy versus the competition's, and how to engage stakeholders for advocacy, philanthropy, or volunteerism. Also, as a volunteer board member you do not typically have any kind of positional power, so you get to develop your skills of leading through influence, strategic thinking, and relationships."

Why is being a versatile CEO so important? It can help you have a big impact on the bottom line. Before he headed up Howmet Aerospace, John Plant was the CEO of the global auto parts manufacturer TRW. In that job he displayed the kind of versatility required to handle diverse operating situations. When he won the top job at TRW in 2003, the global auto parts industry was humming along. Then, with the financial crisis of 2008, the automotive industry hit the skids as demand dried up and the global economy stalled. TRW—which was headquartered in Livonia, Michigan, and made a variety of technology products, including air bags and stability control systems—saw its stock, which had been trading in the high $20s, fall to $3.60 a share in early 2009. In the first quarter of 2009, the once profitable company reported a loss of $131 million. GM and Chrysler, two of TRW's biggest customers, were teetering on the edge of bankruptcy and were headed for a U.S. government bailout. The Center for Automotive Research, an Ann Arbor think tank, predicted that the possible collapse of the industry could destroy three million U.S. jobs. The outlook, to put it mildly, was bleak.

Plant and his team went to work. Starting in 2009, he withdrew

TRW's financial guidance that he had been sharing with stock analysts, executed numerous rounds of layoffs, including engineers at the company's technical center—the source of much of TRW's innovation—and began closing and restructuring plants to reduce its cost structure in response to an ever-changing market and economy. The retrenchment worked, and by 2010 the bleeding had slowed at TRW. Plant then switched hats and embarked on a growth mode, investing in new products and expanding internationally. At the end of Plant's tenure in 2015, TRW employed more than sixty-five thousand people in approximately 190 major facilities around the world and was ranked among the top ten automotive suppliers globally. That year, TRW was sold to the German auto parts maker ZF Friedrichshafen for $105 a share in a deal that valued the company at $13.5 billion.

What accounts for Plant's versatility? Part of it, of course, can be traced to his innate abilities, but he also worked hard to learn how to straddle different worlds—whether it was cost cutting, growth, marketing, or delivering innovation—and to be effective in those situations. One tip: He says that throughout his career he made it a point to pursue new positions with challenges that made him uncomfortable so he would not find himself pigeonholed as a "one note" manager.

GO DEEP

A varied arsenal of operating skills, while essential for success, is only the first leg of being a versatile leader. The second characteristic is to be a deep, creative thinker. Yes, most of us think of ourselves as deep thinkers, but are we really? How many leaders really know or understand the intricacies of their business? Some take on a "fake it until you make it" mentality, brushing over technical details or not truly understanding the competitive landscape, hoping that others in the organization will explain what needs to be known. We're not saying that every leader has to master at a molecular level the products or services they provide. However, thinking deeply about what makes your organization tick and its different capabilities and assets is key to being a versatile leader.

Mastering the details of a company's business might seem a daunting task for a CEO running a high-tech or biotech company, especially if they rose through the ranks via finance or marketing. Yes, a formal education in a particular discipline certainly helps, but the lack of one shouldn't discourage a leader from buckling down and absorbing the intricacies of the business. The key is to be constantly curious. Consider that Leonardo da Vinci didn't have a formal education. He could barely read Latin or do long division. At one point early in his life, Leonardo thought there might be value in studying, of all things, the tongue of a woodpecker, even though he had no plans to draw or paint one. He never knew where his curiosity would take him, but he never stopped exploring. As Walter Isaacson puts it in *Leonardo*, his biography of the artist-inventor, "The reason he wanted to know is because he was Leonardo: curious, passionate, and always filled with wonder."

You need to summon the energy to constantly question what you know and be eager to learn new things—to engage in deep thinking. Plant displayed this kind of avid curiosity after he left TRW in 2015 and later became the CEO of Arconic and then of Howmet Aerospace, jobs that demanded he dive into the intricacies of an entirely new industry. Howmet, based in Pittsburgh, makes jet engine blades, structural components, and other high-tech parts for commercial and military aircraft, among other product lines. While there are some similarities, the aerospace industry is very different from auto parts in both the technologies and the markets. When Plant switched from auto parts to the aerospace industry, he says he put himself into what he calls "deep thinking mode" to find the solutions to the new challenges he faced. "It really just starts off with a lot of rigor," he explains. "You analyze, decide, and—probably even more important—have the confidence to carry out that decision." If you are rigorous in your analysis, if you really think it through, then you can create a path forward for implementation.

Plant began by trying to fathom how the aerospace industry differed from the auto industry. It wasn't only that the products were dissimilar—jet turbine blades versus air bags—but that the applications for the products and the customers were different too. "It's all about intellectual curiosity," says Plant. "You have to engage in an in-depth study of the products you make and the technologies that underpin them—not taking it at face value what they are. You also need to determine whether your products address what your customers need." Gaining an understanding of the aerospace business took months of hard work. Plant visited Howmet's facilities and debriefed employees, often asking the same question of several different people. "The key," he says, "is not just understanding 'what' a product does but also 'how' and 'why' it does what it does. You can then take the 'how' and the 'why' and contextualize it. That lets you know what your competitive advantage is—if you have one."

Today Plant is fully conversant with Howmet's product lineup. At a recent industry event, he stood before an audience and talked about his company's technology—including the differential characteristics of a turbine blade—for more than two hours. A member of the audience, impressed by the CEO's in-depth knowledge, later asked Howmet's CFO if Plant was using a teleprompter. His answer was, "No, he actually knows this stuff."

Plant is not alone in his passion for knowledge. Some the world's most successful leaders are known for being obsessed with the intricacies of their products. At Amazon, Jeff Bezos was watching one of his best software engineers write an algorithm on a whiteboard. He stood up and corrected the formula. Tesla's Elon Musk is known for being able to discuss cutting-edge battery technology and how to develop and integrate powertrains into electric cars. These people, however, tend to be the exception. More typically, leaders shy away from trying to master new areas of thought. Why? In our experience, some simply aren't intellectually curious; others are afraid to fail; and others still don't want to dedicate the required time and energy.

Plant also spent a lot of time trying to understand his competitive advantage on an array of Howmet Aerospace products. He asked himself what his products had that the competition didn't. His ultimate goal: to extract value and charge premium prices or raise existing ones. And at the same time, he wanted to increase market share without his products becoming commodities. In one instance, one of his top customers demanded that he cut the price of one of Howmet's turbine blades. Because Plant had deeply parsed the "how" and the "why" of this product, he was confident that his turbine blade was the best on the market and refused to cut the price. His customer walked away, but Plant didn't fold. "You have to be iron willed to say, 'Okay, then may your God go with you and enjoy yourself.'" Eventually that customer returned and agreed to pay the higher price because their new supplier was unable to meet their very exacting requirements. Plant agreed to provide the part but insisted on a bigger order and an even higher price than before. The customer agreed. Plant hadn't been 100 percent sure that the other supplier couldn't deliver what the customer wanted, but because he had deeply studied the "how" and the "why" of his product, he was fairly confident that his wayward customer would return.

What Plant did when negotiating with this customer is not common practice in the aerospace industry. Generally, suppliers cave to the demands of the big players. Plant says that being new to the industry allowed him to take a fresh approach. He made it a point not to get caught up in the hardwired traditions and practices of aerospace. As he explains, "I decided not to join the secret society. In any major industry, there's always a group of people who are imbued with certain ways of doing business. My courage to change some of the things I did might have been impaired if I was willing to take their advice or get too acquainted with established business practices. If I wanted to be invited to certain forums, then I would need to behave in a certain way, and I didn't want to be forced to behave in that way. The dues were too high to join the club."

One of the characteristics of deep learning is the ability to balance a thirst for knowledge with a sense of certainty. Especially during the first few years of a CEO's tenure, the desire to prove yourself is strong. After all, no one wants to follow leaders who keep changing their minds for no good reason, nor ones who, by contrast, think they have all the answers. When Ed Bastian was appointed Delta Air Lines CEO in 2016, he says he wanted to prove he belonged and that he was equipped to take the job, but it took a couple of years before he felt comfortable in his role. "The CEO job is intimidating and it's humbling. I was responsible for a hundred thousand employees and two hundred million customers a year, and I asked myself, 'How did I get here and did the board make the right decision?' These are things you won't ever admit publicly but internally you have to wrestle with."

Continues Bastian, "The way you deal with this uncertainty is you learn, learn, learn. I went out and saw people to ask them questions, because I really wanted to be the best I could be. And I really do believe that the only thing that is constant is change, and as CEO you need to

get comfortable with change and embrace change. It's constant awareness of maintaining flexibility, maintaining readiness, and being prepared for disruption—both at a micro level and at a macro level for
the long term. That's the way we constantly improve our resilience. In
fact, being CEO is the only job in the company where you have to be
thinking at least five years ahead. Looking ahead over such long time
frames and imagining modifications to the business model and to customer offerings is essential to reinvention, both individually and insti-
tutionally."

When the COVID-19 pandemic hit in early 2020, Bastian put his
philosophy of learning to the test. "Every day we were learning something that contradicted what we thought we knew the day before," he
recalls. "What we needed to do to navigate the pandemic was to keep
taking our business model apart and putting it back together in different ways while continuing to lead through a crisis. It was hard because
you had to be vulnerable. But I'll tell you it was that vulnerability that
helped us rally our employees and customers around us to get through
that period. I let people know that I didn't have the answers, but that I
was committed to working with them to learn and find the answers. It's
far more powerful to say you don't know than you do know. I believe
that using your vulnerability to pull people together adds to your authority as CEO."

In the early days of the pandemic, for example, Bastian was hearing
all sorts of confusing and contradictory information about how to keep
his employees and passengers safe. Is the virus transmitted by air or by
touch? Do masks work, and which ones? Can the ventilation systems on
planes help reduce exposure to the virus? Should the airline mandate
vaccines? While most leaders followed the ever-changing CDC guidelines as best they could, Bastian took the unusual step of reaching out to
one of the country's premier medical establishments, the Mayo Clinic,

and working closely with its top officials to better understand the behavior of the virus. Eventually he even hired Mayo executive Dr. Henry Ting to become Delta's first chief health officer. As one doctor at Mayo put it to him, "The only thing I can tell you, Ed, is that whatever you think you know today, it's going to be different tomorrow." "When I heard that," recalls Bastian, "I realized that he was telling me that you always have to be willing to listen to what can change and learn from it, and that as long we had that mindset, we'd be okay." So in essence, Bastian's fast learning and iterative action cycles created constantly improving standards and practices that protected the health of the airline's passengers and employees.

Bastian's dedication to learning without fear and biases, his willingness to question and rethink long-held beliefs and assumptions, and his ability to study on the fly and learn from the right group of experts helped Delta not only navigate through the turbulence of the pandemic but also come out of the crisis still on top of the industry. Under Bastian's leadership, Delta is America's most-awarded airline. *The Wall Street Journal* declared Delta the best U.S. airline of 2023, the carrier's third consecutive win and its sixth in seven years.

KNOW WHEN TO KEEP SILENT

As we've seen, the ability to assume different operating roles and garner deep knowledge about one's business are two key elements in being a versatile leader. A third—and one that has taken on increasing importance—is having the skills to communicate where a business stands politically, socially, and on environmental issues. At the many Bower Forums we've run, this topic gets constantly raised. Attendees ask, when is it proper to take a stance? Does the CEO speak for the company, or do they need to get a signoff from the board and investors? What if the personal beliefs of the CEO conflict with a position that is in the best interests of the employees and other stakeholders? How do you handle the blowback from taking stances on controversial environmental and social issues? Those who are tempted to publicly embrace progressive issues might remember NBA star Michael Jordan's line: "Republicans buy sneakers, too."

In the current environment, however, neutrality is no longer a viable option. In many instances, leaders must make their beliefs clear in order to build an authentic mandate to rule. Otherwise, employee and customer backlash can be swift and costly. Leaders must ask themselves, "Should I launch this product or that product? Should I select or promote this person if their values don't quite fit with my own? Are my operations harming the community in ways I can avoid?" Leaders know that these situations sometimes create very tough trade-offs where they must forgo lucrative opportunities that are not consistent with the moral compass of their company.

For example, do you stop doing business in Russia in the wake of that country's invasion of Ukraine, or is your business there critical to the well-being of Russian citizens? Do you believe in climate change, and if so, are your zero carbon targets credible or just greenwash?

The temptation is to keep silent and hope the problem disappears. Don Hewitt, the legendary creator of CBS's *60 Minutes*, was once asked what he would do if the press called him. He joked, "Hang up!" After all, taking a stance can sometimes harm a company—some politicians are now targeting businesses they consider "woke" and have sought punitive measures ranging from boycotts to legislation.

The world no longer works this way. You must find a balance, because staying silent all the time is no longer an option in a world where social media scrutiny runs rampant. As Dan Vasella, the former CEO of Novartis and a Bower Forum coach, puts it, "Journalists have a legitimate demand for access to the CEO. But you must modulate that to avoid overexposure. To the media, you are a product. And the press will paint you as either a hero or a villain—whatever sells. So if they paint you as a hero today, you should be prepared to be painted as a villain tomorrow. Not everything you do will work out every time, and you have to accept that people will be unfair." As Vasella suggests, it's wise to limit the times when you should speak out. While of course it doesn't make sense to tweet in response to every headline or employee concern, CEOs need to establish guidelines on when to speak out and when to keep silent on a controversial issue. We've concluded that CEOs should only take a public stance on a topic when it is both relevant to the company and authentic.

Delta Air Lines CEO Bastian, for example, decided that some social issues are just too important to his employees for him to ignore. In the spring of 2021, Georgia passed a law that restricted voting access in the state. He and others saw it as an effort to suppress Black voter turnout. It wasn't an easy decision for Bastian to speak out against the law, but he did. "There are times," he says, "when you find yourself thrust into a topic that has relevance to your people, to your business, and to your local community, and people look to you for an opinion as to what's happening." In this case the voting law was especially relevant: Delta is the largest private employer in the state of Georgia, and it is committed to closing the diversity gaps at leadership and all levels of the company to create an equitable business. At first, Bastian did try to stay above the fray, but as he listened to the increasing concerns of his employees and members of the community, he decided to speak out. "I couldn't explain to them why the law was something we should support. It simply didn't reflect our values, and there was a lot of pressure to take a stand. When

I looked around, everyone in the local corporate community was reluctant to take a stance, and so I felt an obligation to oppose the law."

Many took umbrage with Bastian's stance, but a lot of people agreed with it. After he spoke out, hundreds of CEOs around the country voiced their opposition to the law. Looking back on the situation, Bastian says, "Did it change anything? No, the law is still on the books. But we showed that we had a voice that mattered, and consumers give business to companies who have and practice values."

As Bastian discovered, getting involved in politics can be difficult and stressful, especially in a big corporation whose business interests and constituents might be split on the topic. The challenge is finding the stance and the right language in complex and controversial situations. We believe that there are basic, common shared values on which any CEO or nonprofit leader should always take a stand. These include the protection of innocent life and the condemnation of terroristic, murderous actions. Those are not choices. Those are musts. Yet weighing in on specific policy choices doesn't, in our opinion, make sense unless, as in the case of Delta, the issue is truly relevant to your people and your community. So our advice is to speak out if it's about a commonality of values but think twice when it's policy related.

While leaders must consider all their constituents, it is still the CEO's role to create value for investors. Some investors want companies to adhere to Environmental, Social, and Governance (ESG) factors. Others might be indifferent to those issues and simply want a healthy return. In considering whether and in what way they should express a view, CEOs need to know their shareholders and try to balance their needs while at the same time considering customers, employees, and other constituents. It's not easy. For example, as of the writing of this book, the consensus around the primacy of ESG issues has frayed. While the ESG label itself has become perhaps less useful because it has become politicized, the underlying elements are still important. Leaders need to be versatile enough to know what matters to themselves and to their company, and how to signal the importance of these issues while reframing them in a way that is more relevant to all stakeholders, including employees, outside investors, and politicians.

One practice that helps is to think of the long-term impact of your decision. Will *not* taking a stance hurt the value of the company in the long run—even if speaking out means taking a short-term financial hit? "Is it a view that will stand the test of time when your successor arrives?" asks Howmet's Plant. "Will the new leadership take on that mantle and those views, or are those views likely to be changed by the people who are running the company? Are you putting your successors in a position where there's an expressed view of your company, which they don't own?"

Plant, who was a director at Alcoa and at Masco, says he's been in board meetings where the CEO said he wanted to comment publicly on, say, climate change. One of the directors replied, "Why? Will it help us sell any more cans of paint?" It's one thing to feel strongly about an issue, but if getting involved doesn't add value, why step into the controversy? If you, however, believe that *not* making a statement about an environmental issue will prevent the company from, say, attracting and retaining the best talent, then marshal the evidence to back your argument and present it to the board.

Too often CEOs say they champion environmental issues, or LGBTQ rights, or freedom of speech, but do the company's actions back up those ideals? If you've decided to become involved in a controversial issue, ask yourself whether that decision is authentic and whether the world will perceive it that way. It's easy to say the right thing, but if your organization isn't ready or able to allocate the time and the money to follow through, you can open yourself up to accusations of hypocrisy.

Take the most talked-about of causes in corporate America today: climate change. Many well-meaning leaders have pledged that their company will be net zero carbon by, say, 2030 or 2040, but do they really know how they're going to get there? Of course, if a company has a definite plan to decarbonize and has invested significant funds for it, that's one thing. But that kind of deep commitment tends to be the exception. Often, companies that announce a zero carbon goal fail to engage in a serious decarbonization effort. This opens them up to charges of greenwashing. At Howmet Aerospace, Plant takes a different and what he feels is a more authentic approach to climate change. He refuses to make a net zero commitment for 2030 or 2050 because he doesn't think doing so is credible, or in his words, "It's no more than fluff. People make those commitments," he goes on, "but they don't really mean it, because they don't know how to do it. They won't even be in the job by 2030, never mind by 2050, right?"

Instead, Plant tells his employees and anyone else who asks that Howmet's obligation is not to pollute the air, not to pollute the water, and not to cause any harm to the people who come after them, and that their children and their grandchildren should be able to live in a clean environment. In practice, that means that Howmet puts tens of millions of dollars behind making its manufacturing more efficient and cutting carbon wherever it can along its entire value chain. "All those grand statements about going zero carbon are just political theater," says Plant. "If you don't back them up with real action, you're an empty suit. You have to be authentic; you have to believe what you say, and you have to express a set of values. If you want to take people along with you, you've got to be honest with them."

A s we've seen, trying to navigate the external world can be a mine-field for CEOs. This especially holds true for the new CEOs who attend the Bower Forum who don't have deep experience communicating with outsiders. At one session a new CEO was feeling at a loss when trying to explain his company's stance on a number of issues to his external stakeholders. "When do you speak out and when do you decide that silence is a virtue?" he asked. "Will my stakeholders believe what I say and be willing to help solve my problems?" Fisher of Cincinnati Children's suggests thinking deeply about your mission, your core stake-holders, and which issues you have the legitimacy to weigh in on and that reflect your expertise. "At Cincinnati Children's," recalls Fisher, "we had a pretty good sense of which issues mattered most to children's health, and so speaking up about vaccinations was important for us, but speaking up about climate change, while something we cared about, was probably not one that we felt we needed to be front and center on. We worked with our board to anticipate what could be some of the big public policy and public relations issues that were enduring or likely to emerge over the next six to twelve months and then we'd have our position statements and plans of action ready if we needed them."

When a crisis hits or an important issue arises, many CEOs don't know where to turn. "One of my many mentors," says Fisher, "told me that it's always good to have relationships before you need them, and so I do think a CEO needs to have enough peripheral vision to know which institutions and stakeholder relationships will be important depending on the curveballs that come in life." The key is to invest time in build-ing relationships with customers, employees, the community, and elected officials—*before* you need their help. You should get to know them well enough so you can reach out to them personally in a pinch and not just through surrogates. If the relationships are strong enough, explains Fisher, when there is an issue or a crisis, they might even call you before things get out of hand and offer you some constructive advice or help you maneuver in a tricky situation.

During the COVID pandemic Fisher decided to require vaccinations for all employees—something he knew would not be well received by some health care workers who were reluctant to get the shots. At the time, other hospitals in the region came to the same conclusion. Fisher, having long established good relationships with each of the CEOs, orchestrated a joint announcement of their decision to mandate COVID vaccinations. He believes that joint message helped mitigate some of the uncertainties from employees because it in effect said, "Look, we're all united to provide the safest environment and best health care to the residents of our community, and we've all looked at our own institutions and decided this is important." That's the power of being part of an ecosystem versus just doing things yourself.

While this book is not about personal well-being, we've seen over the years that trying to find the right work/life balance can be very stressful. When your job is demanding and time consuming, it's normal to worry whether you're spending enough time with family and friends. When you're feeling their pull on your time and attention, it's hard to be your best at work and at home. A decade or so ago, experts prescribed a strict work/life balance. The idea was to compartmentalize your work life from your personal life by setting sharp boundaries—in other words, leave your work worries at the office when you're at home and vice versa. The world has changed since then. In the aftermath of the pandemic, many people now work at home at least a day or two a week, if not more. And the increasing use of emails, texts, and video conferencing outside normal business hours has blurred that line even further. Today there really is no hard line between work and life.

Everyone has their own way of dealing with their work/life balance. Over the last few years, however, we've noticed a few patterns. The best leaders first understand and are honest about what interferes with their work and life and find ways to manage those situations. Next, they know that there's a common purpose that maps to both their personal and work lives—that they feel less stressful when they're not trying separate work from their personal life. Finally, they know that energy is more important than time, that being mentally present with your friends or family for short periods is better than spending lots of time with them when you're distracted. With that in mind, we wanted to share with you some stories of leaders who found their own equilibrium when dealing with work/life issues.

Daniel Vasella has an interesting twist on family time. Like many, he tried as much as possible to have breakfast and dinner with his family, limiting his business meals to lunches. However, he used his hour-and-a-half commute home from headquarters in Basel, Switzerland, to speak by phone with his wife, discussing what happened during the day so that when he arrived home for dinner at 8:00 p.m. they didn't have to catch up. "It's difficult for many people to disconnect when they get home. Your head is still in the business or you're on the phone looking at your emails. The family sees you as preoccupied and emotionally unavailable. Because I had that call with my wife, it was as if I had already been home for an hour. That call allowed me to unlink from business."

Lynn Elsenhans, the former CEO of the oil company Sunoco, believes that the most crucial thing is to have a supportive family. "I tell younger women that the most important decision that they will make in their life is who their life partner will be because it is really difficult to go to the highest levels in these corporations if you do not have a supportive partner. It's tough to find that right person. I've been married to the same person for more than forty years, so I was lucky to find that right person."

Managing technology can go a long way toward finding that balance between work and one's personal well-being: "Our phones and other devices have been incredible in improving our productivity, but they also keep us from being fully present," says one executive. Every morning he spends the first forty-five minutes after waking up not touching his phone. Instead he connects with his wife, discussing the upcoming day, listening to Indian music, and having a cup of tea. "I find this time together," he says, "incredibly valuable and it really sets the tone for me for the rest of the day. My advice to everybody is to spend the first half an hour or forty-five minutes on things that give you meaning and allow you to be fully present. It will help you through the day."

Some, like Eddie Ahmed, who runs the international division for MassMutual, find building a successful career so all-encompassing, they don't even attempt to separate work from life—a stance that many, especially the millennial generation who tend to favor life over work, would find unpalatable. "Since I started working in my twenties, I've had a perspective that work and life just blend together. I have always felt that my work flows into my personal life, and my personal life flows into work. I don't think I've taken a real vacation day in over twenty-five years. It's not that I don't take vacation days, but I always end up doing some work. I do not espouse that others do that. I tell my people to take their vacations and put their phones away and not email. It's just not the way I've operated. I'm very comfortable knowing when I need to take time off and reflect. It doesn't have to be defined by a scheduled week or a month off. I'll just do it."

As an example, Ahmed says that after a board meeting in Boston he flew to Los Angeles to spend forty-eight hours climbing the Half Dome rock formation at Yosemite National Park with his twenty-five-year-old son, and then hopped on a plane to London for another meeting. "I was able to do what I thought was really quality stuff with my son and at the same time I didn't miss a heartbeat of my work. It's a blend that brings it all together for me."

Sometimes we feel like we're spinning out of control because there simply isn't enough time to get everything done at work—never mind spending more time with family and friends. If time is a leader's most precious asset, why do so many delegate the use of it to others? Anju Patwardhan, the former head of a Chinese fintech fund, found herself spending too much time coordinating her calendar. Although she had an assistant, she found the countless back-and-forth juggling of her schedule to be both exhausting and not the best use of her time. One day, she was complaining about this to a Chinese CEO who employed forty thousand around the globe, and he told her that he managed his own calendar. When she asked why he didn't use his assistant for scheduling, he replied, "The most valuable thing is my time, and I want to manage my own time. I want to decide what gets prioritized and what doesn't." Patwardhan started running her own calendar for external meetings, and she soon found it much more convenient. "Sometimes when an opportunity to meet with someone comes up on short notice, I know if it's important enough for me to start my day at 7:00 a.m. instead of 8:00, or whether I should switch something out. I can do that much faster than my assistant because I know which day I can work late at night, which day I have a board meeting I can't miss, and what's essential and what's not. Otherwise, I'd lose three days of my assistant trying to coordinate everything."

While we find some of these techniques helpful, they go only so far in addressing what we believe to be the root cause of the stress incurred from trying to maintain a balance between work and family. What we've learned from listening to countless CEOs is one simple lesson. If you're not happy at work, chances are you won't be happy at home. Someone who is miserable at the office might spend lots of time with their family, but how satisfying could that time be if the person is worried, troubled, or depressed? A person who's passionate about their work might not be able to spend much time with their family, but when they do, chances are it will be quality time because they are happy, excited, and feel good about what they are doing. Family members can read your mood, and if it's dark, those vibes will color your relationships. If you come home proud of what you accomplished that day, you've upped your chances of spending quality time with your loved ones.

We've also learned that this works the other way as well. Having solid relationships at home can help you in your job. It's a mutually re-inforcing cycle—a positive feedback loop. For one CEO, this insight helped him salvage his career. He shared how he was struggling because he had divorced his wife, who was having an affair, and he had taken custody of his three children, whose ages spanned from seven years old to fifteen. He told the group that "it was all getting to be too much" and that he was thinking of quitting his job. One member at the session talked about how important it was to have supportive loved ones at home and how to use that energy in one's daily work. After leaving the Forum, the divorced CEO gave deep thought to what he had heard. He started to see his family as a source of strength, and he found a way to use that love at home to power his work at the office. Before long, he found a new spouse who was very caring and helped reduce the strain of being a single parent, which allowed him to continue his journey as a successful CEO.

*Questions to help you develop
your versatility:*

///

- What new versatility skills and experiences do I need to develop and in which assignments and roles can I acquire them?

- What new areas, experiences, training programs, or opportunities for reflection should I consider?

- What are my approaches to learning, and which team members and experts do I need to work with so I can learn?

- What amount of time do I need to allocate to expand my versatility, both for on-the-job learning and in-depth study?

///

*Questions to help you know when to
take a stance and when not to:*

//

- Does getting involved in a public topic or controversy actually add value to the company?

- In considering whether or not I should express a view, have I balanced the needs of shareholders, customers, employees, and other constituents?

- Are my and our beliefs and values clear enough and have they been shared to the extent that I have an authentic mandate to speak for the company?

//

In Summary

//

With all the accelerating and fewer and fewer predictable changes around geopolitics, technology, supply chains, consumer attitudes, and climate change facing us, being versatile is critical to be a successful leader. Picking a few areas that are most important for you and your organization and going deep is a practice that leaders have to learn. A realization that you are not the smartest person on all topics is foundational for continual learning.

All the suggested new practices in human leadership described in part 1 are designed to help you get to know yourself better and to lead yourself "inside." In part 2, we take a more external view, telling stories of leaders who took what they learned about themselves and then turned to the outside, applying their new human-centric skills to bring about real change in their teams and organizations. In essence, they learned to lead from the inside out and then moved beyond themselves.

Part 2

//

MOVING BEYOND
YOURSELF

7

THE IMPOSSIBLE BEGINS WITH YOU

The leaders who were gathered around the table at a Bower Forum listened as a new CEO complained about her executive team. "I've got my strategy set and I'm ready to execute, but my team doesn't feel passionate about what we're trying to do. Instead, they have questions, excuses, and problems they want to discuss, which is fine—I'm here to listen and decide—but that takes up a lot of our energy. Our strategic plan feels like it's stalled."

One of the more seasoned CEOs at the table asked whether the new leader had defined the company's purpose and set clear goals that align with that purpose. And if so, whether she had been able to engage and excite her team to own those goals jointly. To do so, another CEO chimed in, requires that a leader be crystal clear about how the purpose links to the financial targets that need to be met and then be unforgiving when they're not: "Sure, you can listen to problems, but you've hired your executive team to come up with solutions, not excuses. If they can't do that, you've got the wrong people in those top jobs."

As this CEO discovered, many people in today's workforce look for meaning in their job, and if you cannot create a sense of purpose, even the best-laid strategies will falter. In the last decade or so, we've seen an evolution in the leadership paradigm from a model where you told people what to do and your employees executed your orders to a model where you have to be clear about your own purpose and the purpose of the institution. You have to ask yourself why you want to be a CEO. Who are you trying to serve and what difference are you trying to make for society? Once you've made a conscious choice, you need to lead with purpose and at the same time get your people to understand and embrace that aspiration.

To be effective in this quest, it helps to remember that purpose is not just about you. Successful leaders have a clear view of the world and a purpose that goes well beyond themselves. They recognize what the world needs in order to become a better place and how they can harness the power of their organization to move toward that change. Only then can they mobilize institutions and bring about real change.

In part 2 of this book, we take a more external view, telling stories of leaders who took what they learned about themselves and applied it to bring about real change in their organizations. In this chapter, we explore the seventh element of the process, "Embed Purpose." We ask leaders to think about defining purpose and helping their employees to develop a strong sense of *why* they come to work each day. Of course, some companies have an easier job of this than others. If you run a solar energy or an organic food company, you can rally the troops around fighting climate change or helping people live healthier lives. Former Unilever CEO Paul Polman inspired his employees at the food and personal care giant by stressing the difference they could make by selling products in the developing world that emphasized healthy living. Yvon

Chouinard, the founder of outdoor gear maker Patagonia, made the environment a core part of the company's mission and values. This helped create a strong sense of purpose and meaning among Patagonia employees, who feel that they are contributing to a larger cause by working for the company.

But what if you're running a business such as ball bearings or auto parts that doesn't on the face of it seem to have an inspiring purpose? Those products hardly make most people's hearts flutter. That's exactly the dilemma that Delphi CEO Rodney O'Neal faced when he was in the midst of one of the biggest and what eventually became one of the most successful turnarounds in corporate history.

In 1999, after GM spun off its Delphi auto parts division, the newly independent company stood as one of the biggest suppliers in the industry, making, among other things, products for infotainment, safety, electrical wiring systems, and electronics in thirty countries. Delphi, though, struggled under the weight of bloated costs, sclerotic middle management, stringent union contracts, and poor morale. At one point, because of union rules, the company had to keep unneeded workers on the payroll, and they sat in the cafeteria every day—at a cost to Delphi of $1 billion a year. In 2005, the company declared bankruptcy, and two years later, O'Neal, who had been president, assumed the CEO title.

Although bankruptcy released Delphi from those onerous union contracts and freed up the core business to grow, a brutal path lay ahead. Most companies don't make it out of bankruptcy—there's a good reason they end up there in the first place—and O'Neal's executive team had been beaten down by years of running a company that was hemorrhaging money. They had no passion and no sense of direction. The first thing he did was get in a room with his direct reports and establish a clear strategic plan that they all agreed upon. On the surface, the plan was simple: shed a long list of commodity products and invest in R&D to make high-value products with a competitive advantage. The complicated part was executing that plan.

O'Neal knew that the psychological well-being of his executive team mattered, and he wanted to instill in them a sense of pride and have them be passionate about what they were doing. He knew the importance of psychological support. He grew up poor and Black in Dayton, Ohio, with parents who cared about education. He attended college at the General Motors Institute and became an engineer who had to fight his way up the hierarchy at the automaker, where he says he wouldn't have made it without the strong support of a mentor named Bill. As he recalls, "No matter how much I sometimes struggled with the vastly different culture, the loneliness, the sense of isolation as an African American, Bill managed to keep me there, advising me to stay and change things instead of quitting. It has always been my good fortune to have been surrounded and supported by individuals who cared about me, people who unselfishly lifted me on their shoulders and carried me to success across the abyss of failure." So he applied some of that same psychological support to his team. He turned up the heat, arguing that they could become the best of the best. He explained how bankruptcy could be a positive tool rather than a black badge, and that now they had the opportunity to work for a company that actually made money.

But there was more: Everything was going to change. O'Neal knew that he wasn't going to be able to execute his ambitious strategy unless his team woke up in the morning psyched to go to work. A turnaround is backbreaking and sometimes demoralizing work. The CEO needed a rallying cry that would help his team feel that they were making a difference in the world. After lengthy discussions with the team, O'Neal arrived at Delphi's motto. It was to make products that were "safe, green, and connected." The phrase was simple but powerful. "Safe" evoked the idea that the parts Delphi made would protect the families and children who drove cars with Delphi parts on board. "Green" was a challenge to manufacture parts with the lowest possible carbon footprint and pitch in on the battle against climate change. "Connected" referred to the burgeoning use of microchips and software in cars. It was a challenge to his team to become the most technologically sophisticated company in its industry. The beauty of the phrase was that it stressed the global nature of Delphi's business. "The idea," recalls O'Neal, "was that our products would appeal across national boundaries. No matter where they live in the world, everyone wants a vehicle that's safe, green, and connected."

Once O'Neal knew where he wanted to go, he had to figure out how to get there. "The key to any radical revolution," he says, "is to get the people to do what they say they're going to do. Do not come back and tell me you can't push ahead, because if you can't, we have to get somebody who can." At the time, he saw signs of recession in the air. He had traveled to Washington often and had gotten wind of a global financial system that was out of kilter. O'Neal knew he had to move fast. The economy was showing signs of stress, and the meltdown that would become known as the financial crisis of 2008 was about to hit. GM, which would file for bankruptcy in 2009, accounted for 60 percent of Delphi's global business. If Delphi was to survive, it would have to expand globally, winning increasingly more business from foreign carmakers that would be attracted to their cutting-edge products.

O'Neal had listened to his team, and working with them helped them to articulate a shared sense of purpose. Now he had to balance the humility and patience he had displayed when unearthing that shared passion with the courage to act decisively. He first suggested that his team use their new sense of purpose as a guide. That meant scrapping any product that didn't meet the "safe, green, and connected" mantra. Then, sitting with his executive team, O'Neal laid out a set of extreme stretch goals. He wanted Delphi to have the highest profit margins and return on invested capital in the business. That's a tall order for any business, never mind one that had been losing money for years. And it meant a lot of tough love. Most leaders want to be liked. It's only human nature. O'Neal believes that respect is more important. He used his force of personality to remind his team that there were no excuses, and he summoned the courage to do this consistently. It was the only way he knew to build high-level execution into the culture: "You give your management team a number, and they have to hit it. That was the difference between my management team and others. Anybody can put all this stuff in a PowerPoint presentation and it all sounds good. Very few can actually execute what they present on the screen." Trying to meet such stretch goals can be stressful and exhausting. However, the sense of purpose that O'Neal instilled in his team helped them keep drilling away day after day.

Not everyone in the organization could meet O'Neal's "no excuses" leadership style. This presented a dilemma. How do you balance being inspirational, respected, and liked while holding people to extremely high standards and then firing them if they fail? "When somebody is not doing what they're supposed to be doing and you remove them," explains O'Neal, "the way you do it has to be ethical and fair." The key was no surprises. The CEO says he didn't have to give his reports annual reviews because he was completely transparent and let them know where they stood every day. "By the time I had to fire someone," he says, "everyone else on the team would say, 'You know what? That person deserved it.' You have to be judicial about how you use power." Consider the opposite situation, where a leader wants to be liked and therefore doesn't fire an underperformer in a timely manner. That kind of behavior can have a negative impact on the other teammates, who will surely resent a colleague who's not pulling their weight and might end up resenting the leader for not acting.

O'Neal also applied a full transparency policy to the company's financials. Typically, corporations keep two sets of books, one that sets ambitious internal financial goals and another for Wall Street, which seeks more attainable goals. O'Neal's extreme goals were one and the same—the financial goals he shared with investors were the same for his executive team. And those numbers had to conform to the "safe, green, and connected" mantra as a guiding strategic principle for Delphi's product portfolio. "We had one number," says O'Neal, "and that number was one that my executives gave to me—one that they thought they could achieve. So if the plan stalled, I'd say, 'Don't come to me saying you're not going to hit your number, because I approved the capital for you to reach your goal and that's what's driving my return on investment and my margins. This is why I gave you the money four years earlier, so don't tell me you can't get there.' It's not a question of what will get done; it's only a question of who will do it."

Of course, O'Neal did everything in his power to help his team hit their numbers. Often, strategic plans change, priorities shift, and tactics get deployed that don't support the larger strategic plan or conform to the company's purpose. To avoid that, O'Neal kept his team laser focused on achieving the highest ROI and margins in the industry. For example, at the time it would have been tempting to enter fast-growing markets such as India and Russia, but O'Neal concluded that he couldn't make sufficient profits there, so Delphi stayed out. At the same time, he upped R&D spending dramatically, focusing on high-end products that the competition would have a hard time duplicating. Delphi used to hand out awards to engineers and researchers who invented something cool like four-wheel steering, even if it didn't catch on in the marketplace. Now awards went only to those who invented a feature that sold well and had high margins. "We didn't want to be on every car," says O'Neal, "we only wanted to be on upscale, sophisticated cars, with products that are safe, green, and connected. You have to understand what business you're in and where you sell and stay true to that. No matter how good our technology, if it was on a car that didn't sell, we didn't make any money."

O'Neal's plan worked, and Delphi became very profitable. But that doesn't mean he stopped there. He had to keep up the pressure for excellence. "When we get there," says O'Neal, "we're going to stay there. And that's how you get great, because greatness is defined by staying there." It's easy for any company to slip once it's on top, because the leadership can get too comfortable. When that happens, the competition sees the amount of money being made, and they come in and start competing in areas they hadn't competed in before. O'Neal pushed his team to keep innovating, cannibalizing their current lineup of products with more advanced offerings. He also found creative ways to motivate his team. One day he told an employee that he wanted everyone to be a honey badger, a fierce animal. For a joke, O'Neal sent out a video of a honey badger going after his prey, and it went viral inside the company. Before long, managers were hanging photos of the creatures on their office walls.

By the time he stepped down as CEO in 2015, O'Neal had raised Delphi's margins to the high teens in an industry where single-digit margins were the norm. His return on capital hit 30 percent, and the stock—from the time Delphi IPO'ed in 2011 to his stepping down as CEO in 2015—had quadrupled.

This might seem like hard-nosed, numbers-driven capitalism, but O'Neal rationalizes his approach: "The only reason you exist is to make money, and when you make money then you can do good things for society, provide for your employees, and make the world a better place.

When we opened factories in developing countries, we left the water and air cleaner than when we got there. The people there went from subsistence farming to good-paying factory jobs. And all that was only possible if I kept doing what I was doing and hit my numbers."

While using purpose as a motivator is a crucial part of good leadership, sometimes it's not clear exactly what that purpose should be. Some employees, especially among the millennial and Gen-Z cohorts, are looking for more—but what is it exactly that they want? When hiring and then motivating her people, Claire Babineaux-Fontenot, the CEO of Feeding America, always searches for the "why." She engages in open and frank conversations to understand their purpose and intentions. The job of the leader is to listen to what their people want to get out of life, and then find a way to link that sense of purpose to the strategy of the business.

Earlier in her career, when Babineaux-Fontenot was the chief tax officer at Walmart, she had set some brutal stretch goals for tax efficiency and needed to get her team pumped up for the challenge. It's hard to feel passionate about helping a giant corporation save money on its taxes, but Babineaux-Fontenot found a way. "I had conversations with members of the team," she recalls, "who clearly were asking themselves, 'Why does this even matter? At our core what do we really do in the tax department?'" The answer that Babineaux-Fontenot and her team arrived at after some long, heartfelt conversations was that by lowering costs for Walmart they actually help Walmart to deliver on its promise of "everyday low cost for consumers," which means that people can save money and live better. It worked. As we learned in chapter 5, Babineaux-Fontenot and her team hit those stretch tax targets, saving a considerable sum for both Walmart and its customers.

At Walmart, Babineaux-Fontenot soon started reexamining her own "why." She was diagnosed with cancer, which suddenly put her life in an entirely new perspective. She had a successful career but felt that something was missing. Growing up, she had seen people from her poor community who, against steep odds, had given back and helped others. Deep within, she knew that one day she wanted to give back to society the same way so many in her community, including her parents, had done, but she always told herself there was plenty of time to do that. When cancer hit, it reminded her of her long-held promise in the most profound way. "With death facing me, I could no longer trick myself into thinking I would always have more time down the road to be useful. The course that I was on at Walmart was not going to help me to realize my dream of profoundly giving back to society." Many of her friends and colleagues tried to dissuade her, saying that everybody feels lost because of the great shock that comes with cancer, and it's unwise to make any rash decisions. But she had connected deeply with her "why," and after five surgeries and seemingly endless chemotherapy sessions, her cancer went into remission, and she left Walmart. She soon became the CEO of Feeding America. "The first year of being CEO," she recalls, "I apologized nearly every time I met people who had worked in the nonprofit space for most of their careers. I said, 'I'm so sorry it took me so long.'"

While it seems obvious that anyone working for an outfit like Feeding America already has a built-in "why," Babineaux-Fontenot would nonetheless test for the strength and the depth of it in her employees. That's because the job could challenge even those who strongly believed in eradicating hunger, something that was especially true during the COVID-19 pandemic.

Early on in the pandemic, when nobody knew much about COVID, the people at Feeding America had to make life-and-death decisions nearly every day. They were on the front lines trying to feed people, and the advice coming out of government agencies was confusing at best. First you didn't need masks, then you did need a mask but a cloth one would do—you didn't need an N-95. Then, oops, you did need an N-95 mask. Babineaux-Fontenot had to put people's lives in danger by sending them out into the field, and in fact many of her employees contracted COVID while out feeding those who needed to be fed. Some died.

Some employees asked Babineaux-Fontenot why they should go out and risk their lives. Before the pandemic started, she would ask both members of her team and new hires why they were here and what they hoped to accomplish. The answers were sincere—most wanted to help their community—but that "why" provided scant comfort during the pandemic. "I had so many tearful conversations with people who were afraid," says Babineaux-Fontenot.

Leading through purpose requires that leaders humble themselves and truly listen to the fears and insecurities that arise when people try to go the extra mile to fulfill that purpose. The best leaders are not only good listeners but flexible enough to see when following the cause starts exacting too high a price on their employees. Babineaux-Fontenot won over her staff by, first, not requiring anyone to go into the field. Next, and more important, she acknowledged their fears and was honest about the fact that there were risks attached to the decisions they were going to be making. "I told them," she recalls, "that they could be good people and answer the call differently. Some, whether because of fear or health reasons, decided not to go to the front lines, but I didn't criticize them for that decision. I embraced them because it was the right decision for them and for their families. I tried to create space for them to be able to make a different decision than some others were making." As for Babineaux-Fontenot, even though she was a cancer survivor with a weakened immune system, she felt that the personal risk from COVID was outweighed by the potential impact she could make by visiting Feeding America's food banks and distribution centers around the country in person, and she had a rule that the one person from the national office who was going to travel throughout the pandemic was the CEO. As of 2024, Babineaux-Fontenot has not tested positive for COVID.

So the best leaders encourage their people to understand their why and then give them the space to decide how it applies to their work. As Babineaux-Fontenot discovered, the vast majority of Feeding America employees risked their health and lives by showing up to feed people facing hunger. They made that decision because she had helped them develop a strong passion for what they were doing. She had help them solve for their "why."

When trying to instill passion and purpose into his team members, BIC CEO Gonzalve Bich likes to tell stories. "One thing that every generation loves—and this is especially true with Gen Z and millennials—is a hero. If you want to inspire Gen Z and millennials, you create heroes, because normally they won't step up to the dais and tell their own stories, but it's my job as a leader to help them be there or have their teammates recognize them for their success and wins." One story that Bich likes to tell that resonates with his employees is about a team of engineers who were stumped by a problem with a machine on one of the production lines. On Monday morning when everyone returned to work, they found the machine running. It turns out the maintenance man had fixed it over the weekend using duct tape and other simple materials sourced from the maintenance storeroom. The story is about dedication, taking the initiative, helping others, and being innovative—all qualities that Bich likes to see in his organization, and he believes that repeatedly talking about those qualities helps reinforce them.

Bich also realized that the up-and-coming generation was very concerned about social equity and climate change and might be reluctant to work for a company that was hurting more than it was helping. For example, before Bich became CEO in 2019, the company needed a better way to explain to job candidates what it was doing about climate change. While BIC had green programs in place, they weren't organized or publicized. You can't talk your way out of these situations—even if the company was already making progress—so after he took the helm, Bich doubled down on the work the company was doing on sustainability. He increased the percentage of recycled materials in his products, set zero-carbon targets for his operations, and set up waste reduction programs. He also pledged that by 2025, all his packaging would be recycled, reusable, compostable, or green—97 percent of BIC lighters are now sold without any packaging. To offer consumers increasingly sustainable options, he also acquired Rocketbook, a company that makes notepads that allow writing to be digitized in a simple way and the notebooks to be reused endlessly.

The key, he says, is to be authentic about the good work you are doing. First, a company can't try to solve every societal issue. Bich picked three points that he thought made the most sense to his brand—safety for his factory workers, sustainability, and giving back to the community with an emphasis on education, the last of which fits with BIC being a writing instrument company. With the environment, Bich didn't set some far-off zero waste or 100 percent recyclable goal—first because it is scientifically impossible and second because the cost would be prohibitive. With BIC razors, for example, you can't eliminate the steel for the blade, and it's not recyclable. You need some plastics for the structural integrity of BIC's lighters, because BIC refuses to compromise consumer safety. Saying that the company strives for 100 percent reductions wouldn't be authentic. Bich set more modest goals—a 50 percent reduction in product waste—and he's very transparent about the amount of capital he spends on sustainability. "Our employees," he says, "like the visibility and accountability, and they're telling us, 'Okay, BIC's not perfect, but the company is doing what it said it was going to do, and we can live with that.' It's amazing to see that linkage between authentic leadership and engaging the new generations' talent."

Sometimes even the best people in an organization can begin to lose their sense of purpose. Typically, these people have done a great job for years or even decades but start to lose their drive and question why they are still there. At the technology service firm Cognizant, then CEO Frank D'Souza found this to be the case with some members of his executive team who had been there for years, were financially independent, and had started to feel burned out. Not wanting to lose his best, most seasoned executives, D'Souza created a very structured program called "Success to Significance." The idea was to have frank and open discussions with the team, exploring whether their jobs were still significant to them, and if not, why? D'Souza designed the program to instill a new sense of purpose.

As part of the program, D'Souza would gather his top team for multiday off-sites with a facilitator who would prompt them to talk about their lives, their hopes, and their desires. They would discuss meaning, authenticity, purpose, and what was significant to them. The program required leaders to be very vulnerable, but it was valuable because it allowed the people in the room to talk about both their personal and their professional journeys, something those in high-powered corporate jobs rarely do. They shared how they grew up, what their parents taught them, how they came to be where they were, and what their biggest failures and biggest successes were. "It led people to have a different and deeper level of caring and compassion for each other, for the business, and for the outcomes that they were generating," says D'Souza. "We created an atmosphere where people felt comfortable and safe. It contextualized that we weren't just doing work for customers, but that what we were doing was part of something much bigger. People who previously looked at each other as just that executive who runs that part of the business suddenly seemed more human to each other, and everyone cared more."

In D'Souza's case, he used one "Success to Significance" event to share his life journey with others on his executive team. "I was nervous telling it," he recalls, "but it was worth it because I think it humanized me as a leader." He recounted how his father was a diplomat who moved every three years and brought D'Souza, his siblings, and his mother along with him, and would enroll the kids in the local schools. That meant that every three years D'Souza had to learn the local language, adjust to the local cuisine, and make new friends. At the off-site, he explained to his colleagues how hard it was to make such frequent moves, but looking back on it he said he wouldn't change a thing. The experience of relocating in foreign lands taught him resilience. With each new culture that he assimilated into, he learned that we are more similar than we are different.

After returning from these sessions, D'Souza found that his top executives—even those who had been at Cognizant for twenty years—approached their work with a renewed sense of energy and purpose. The "Success to Significance" experience helped them become more open, caring, and better team leaders, qualities that started to spread throughout the rest of the organization team by team.

As D'Souza discovered, the question all of us need to ask ourselves is, do we really understand the story of the people we're working with? That means their real background, their fears, and their motivations. To achieve that level of empathy, we need to put more effort into understanding what makes our colleagues tick. Only then can we grow both professionally and personally.

*Questions to help you assess whether
you are driving your organization
toward a clear purpose:*

- Am I clear on what drives my energy and sense of purpose? Can I clearly articulate how that is related to my organization's purpose?

- Do we as a leadership team share a common sense of purpose? Are we aligned on how that guides our decisions?

- How can I better understand what drives the energy and gives meaning to the people I'm working with? How can I use these insights to give our organization meaning and purpose?

- Do we spend the time to make sure this purpose is shared broadly in the organization and that all employees understand how a sense of purpose shows up in their day-to-day work?

- When hiring key employees, how do I engage in more open and frank conversations in order to understand their purpose and their intentions?

- How does living our purpose inform career development in the organization?

In Summary

///

Every human being needs to connect with a sense of purpose to navigate through their own challenging and demanding journey. All great CEOs listen to their constituents and then carefully devise a clear purpose for the organization that inspires both themselves and their people. At times, they will need to use that sense of purpose to help guide them when they are faced with the need for a radical change of direction. The key is to leverage that passion and an unwavering commitment to your organization's purpose when making big, bold moves.

8

TAKE FEAR OUT
OF THE DRIVER'S SEAT

n today's topsy-turvy environment, figuring out what big, bold moves to make and then getting your people to back you with gusto is a tall order. To develop a strong and clear mandate for change, every leader has to think through how to balance competing priorities and intentions. There's short-term performance versus long-term; there's the need to care for your people, but also the need to pressure them to perform. You want to be at the forefront of technology and innovation—which in the case of a technology such as AI/GenAI requires a lot of time and effort to master—but at the same time you understand that it's not going to pay off tomorrow. So leaders need to manage those tensions and the competing priorities.

In our eighth leadership element, we explore the notion that leadership is not just about making decisions. It requires the courage and the confidence to make bold and risky moves when the circumstances require it and then to inspire your team to help you get to where you need to go. This requires that you align your team with the purpose and strategy of the organization and constantly help renew their energy and enthusiasm, while fine-tuning your personal interactions with them.

The reality is that nobody really knows what an organization is going to look like in five years. The best leaders create a system that allows the organization to evaluate bold moves from all angles, then test them out to recognize which of them show the most promise. Sometimes those big moves are unpopular or untested, but nonetheless are worth the risk, because if successful they will yield great dividends, creating a more defendable competitive advantage.

To make bold moves you first have to overcome your own fear that you'll fail, and then persuade others to embark on this high-wire journey with you. If you are hesitant and unsure of the path forward, your team will be too. But if you gather courage and really believe in the new direction you want the organization to take, and you show that you're passionate about the mission, that can be infectious. As Winston Churchill put it, "Before you can inspire with emotion, you must be swamped with it yourself. Before you can move their tears, your own must flow. To convince them, you must yourself believe."

In the business world, big, signature moves can be one-time bets or a series of moves over your tenure as CEO that shape the future of the business. As we have witnessed signature moves over the years, we have seen that they can be internal moves such as implementing a new organizational model, creating a framework for resource allocation, or reinventing your R&D center. Others are external, industry-shaping moves such as M&A, partnerships, product innovation breakthroughs, or new business models. In some situations, courage is needed to *stop* doing something, such as exiting a market, trimming a portfolio, or shutting down an investment.

A classic example is when in 2011 Netflix CEO Reed Hastings, sensing that video streaming was the future, started to deemphasize the company's successful DVD mail-order business. Whatever the case, it takes courage to summon the will to make such a move, and it takes skill to infect your executive team with the same courage, energy, and passion to make that big wager a success.

This book is not about the nuts and bolts of building executive teams. Countless other books have given valuable advice on how to compose a top team by attracting members with a diversity of expertise, a complementary nature of expertise, as well as shared common values, purpose, mutual trust, and operating principles. What we are focused on is how to unleash leadership in your team and in your organization more broadly.

If you're going to ask your executive team to go along with you on your bold journey, you have to instill in them the confidence that they belong—they have to know you have their back. This means providing both emotional and practical support, such as acting as a safe and forgiving sounding board for their thoughts and ideas. In one example, members of an executive team were resisting their CEO because they felt he wasn't empowering them. One team member told the CEO he was worried that he was going to fail on an assignment. The CEO said to him, "I recruited you and cultivated you for six months. I own so much of your success. If you fail, I fail." Sharing that feeling made the CEO appear vulnerable, but once he opened up, his team started to step up and play bigger. They knew he had their back.

Stéphane Bancel, the CEO of Moderna, the company that helped create a COVID-19 vaccine, is someone who made some signature moves under tremendous pressure and got his employees to go on the journey with him. He is a perfect example of our eighth leadership element,

"Inspire Boldness." Although he feared that he might be jeopardizing the future of a company that had many promising lifesaving drugs in the pipeline, he summoned the courage to make some big, bold bets to get the Moderna COVID-19 vaccine onto the market in record time and marshaled his organization to achieve what they thought was impossible.

At first there seemed to be nothing to worry about. In late 2019, a handful of residents of Wuhan, China, came down with a severe respiratory flu and had difficulty recovering. Then the disease started to spread fast. China locked down Wuhan, and officials soon realized they had the beginnings of a deadly pandemic on their hands. On January 11, 2020, Chinese scientists uploaded onto the web the genetic sequence of this never-before-seen coronavirus in the hope that the world medical community would find ways to combat this new scourge.

Ten days after China uploaded the data, Bancel, the CEO of a small American biotech company named Moderna, was attending the World Economic Forum in Davos, Switzerland. Bancel, who had been running the company since 2010, was a chemical engineer with an MBA from Harvard. Previously he had helped run a French biotechnology company, BioMérieux.

At Davos, however, he had more on his mind than global economics. During the 2019 Christmas holidays, Bancel had noticed a short article in *The Wall Street Journal* about an outbreak of a different kind of flu in China that was spreading quickly. Although he had no formal medical training, as the CEO of a biotech company he had throughout his career made it a priority to study infectious diseases. His experience in the pharmaceutical industry told his gut that something was wrong, so Bancel dove deeply into the topic. He had studied the pandemic of 1918 and, using that as context, started to chart the potential spread of this new pathogen. He knew the speed of replication of a virus is exponential and he set up an Excel spreadsheet to predict the spread of COVID. What he saw alarmed him. "I realized that in a month there was a good chance we'd be in a pandemic. The virus had started to pop up in China, in Thailand, and in Japan. Planes with infected people were landing in all the capitals in Asia, all the capitals in Europe, and all the West Coast cities in the U.S."

By the time he was at Davos in late January 2020, Bancel concluded that the situation was even worse than he thought. "I woke up 4:00 a.m. sweating, realizing that this was going to be like a 1918 flu pandemic and millions of people are going to die." The next day he met with numerous officials from public health groups who urged him to work on a COVID-19 vaccine. Because of the work Moderna had done on SARS and MERS—viruses similar to COVID—Bancel believed that Moderna's vaccine technology had a 90 percent chance of working. "So, when you put those two things together—a good chance that the drug would work and the high chance of a pandemic where a lot of people were going to die—I thought to myself, 'All right, let's run!'" That evening, Bancel called Moderna's cofounder Noubar Afeyan, and the two decided on the spot to take the enormous risk of producing in record time a new type of vaccine that could help quell this novel virus.

What gave Bancel the courage to act, to make a move that, if it failed, could bankrupt the company? The deep learning and curiosity that he had about infectious diseases allowed him to develop a substantive view on the risks involved with this big decision that, in turn, led him to be bolder and make a more courageous decision. Another way to look at it—the more you learn, the more curious you are about your business, and the more time you spend deeply thinking about your industry, the more confidence you'll have to make signature moves. As Bancel puts it, "If I hadn't over the last twenty years been studying infectious diseases, including infectious disease history, I would not have been able to connect the dots so quickly that this was going to be like the 1918 epidemic. And if I had not had a deep and detailed knowledge of Moderna's technology, I might not have been able to assess that we had a good chance of making a COVID vaccine work."

The rest of Moderna's story is legend. Only thirty-four days after the two executives made their fateful decision, the company delivered a vaccine to the U.S. Food and Drug Administration for testing. In the following months some thirty thousand volunteers participated in clinical trials, and at the end of 2020, the FDA approved the vaccine for emergency use. Historically, vaccines had taken years if not decades to reach this stage. Moderna did it in less than a year. So far, more than a billion doses of the lifesaving vaccine have been administered around the world. And that's not the only way that Bancel's big moves paid off. In 2020, the company quadrupled its cash on hand to $5.25 billion and generated positive cash flows for the first time in its ten-year history. By early 2024, the company's stock market capitalization sat at $40 billion.

What's less well known is that the bet that Bancel made on that January night at Davos could have spelled the end of his company, which at the time had no revenues, a dwindling cash reserve, and employed eight hundred. Making risky decisions is not easy. Money, jobs, and reputations are on the line. The CEO needed to find ways to overcome his doubts and anxieties to make game-changing, signature moves and to persuade his executive team to come along with him for the ride. He needed to draw on his inner resources to better position the organization for future profitable growth and align his workforce to build a stronger organization.

When Bancel first joined Moderna, it wasn't clear that messenger RNA (mRNA) technology would be viable. Over the next decade, the company experimented with the technology to create vaccines for HIV, cancer, and other diseases but didn't yet have a product on the market when COVID-19 hit. The mRNA in Moderna's vaccines tells cells to create a protein that triggers an immune response that attacks the actual virus. The breakthrough was that the technology can quickly be adjusted and adapted to different medical needs. In a blog post, Judy Savitskaya, a biotech entrepreneur, and Jorge Conde, a general partner at the venture capital firm Andreessen Horowitz, wrote that bio-platforms like Moderna's mRNA technology were to the biotech industry what the assembly line was to the auto industry. "We went from single 'job shops' in the early days of automobiles—where raw materials like steel and rubber [were] crafted from start to finish by hand into a trickle of early cars— to assembly line production, with standard components that could be iterated for new models."

Just about everyone thought Bancel was crazy to even try to make a vaccine—never mind in record time. The company had never before done a phase 3 drug trial, plus it had no employees or infrastructure to manufacture and distribute a new vaccine at scale. His suppliers, competitors, and some of his own employees told him he was wasting his time.

Ignoring his critics, Bancel put Moderna on crisis mode, heading up the COVID-19 vaccine program himself. He didn't care about titles or defined roles. He wanted everyone to own the problem and act fast. The key for Bancel was to build a very entrepreneurial and aggressive company. "We wanted to maximize our impact on patients and feel that every day matters, so we were willing to take calculated risks. When there is no great upside and little downside, that's an easy decision. We wanted Moderna to be much more like a risk-taking tech company than a typical pharmaceutical company."

One of those calculated risks came in the spring of 2020 when Moderna was trying to build the capacity for manufacturing a billion doses of the COVID-19 vaccine and needed significant funding to ramp up. Because of the large amounts of money involved, if the vaccine was to fail, so would this fledgling company. After Bancel approached big foundations and governments for funding to expand manufacturing and came up dry, he decided to go to the public markets in May of that year to raise $1.3 billion. He faced a dilemma, however. The vaccine's phase 1 trial data on safety would not be out for another month. If he waited until the data were available and the results were positive, it would be much easier and cheaper to raise capital. But a month's delay would dramatically reduce the company's manufacturing capacity, and because of the severity of the pandemic, time was of the essence. In his heart, Bancel knew that the welfare of the patient was a priority for Moderna, so he decided to make a signature move. It paid off. He raised the $1.3 billion he needed.

Another signature move Bancel made was deciding to slow down the phase 3 clinical trials, which are designed to prove the effectiveness of the vaccine. The company started phase 3 on July 27, 2020. In the first few weeks, the results were better than expected, but the trials didn't include enough minority volunteers, especially Black Americans, who were being hit particularly hard by COVID-19. The CEO told his team, "Look, if one of the communities that is the most impacted by the virus doesn't believe in the vaccine and doesn't get the vaccine, we will have failed society." So, after a lot of discussions over a few days, Bancel and his team decided to slow down the study to recruit more minorities, which of course was going to delay the approval of the drug. "That was a tough one," he says. "My people have been sweating bullets—sacrificing evenings, nights, weekends—for eight months by the time I had to make the decision. But at the end of the day, I think with all tough decisions, when you step back and you look at the big picture, they actually become easier. It was the right thing to do."

Early in 2020, it still wasn't obvious how serious a threat the virus posed. Bancel had to convince his team that this actually was going to be a global pandemic and, as he put it, "that I was not crazy and seeing something that nobody else was seeing." That took him a few weeks of meetings and lots of persuasion, but he finally got the top of the organization rowing in the same direction, understanding that while they were racing against this virus, every day mattered.

To successfully move from making one hundred thousand doses of the vaccine in 2019 to a billion in 2021, Bancel had to divide the company in two. He created a COVID-19 team and a non-COVID team to keep working on the nearly twenty other drugs Moderna had in the pipeline. Speed was essential, so he started meeting with his COVID executive team once or twice a week instead of the usual once a month. Bancel wanted to run a decentralized organization where everyone took ownership, but he also wanted to make sure his stretch goals were being met. In between the weekly meetings he kept in touch with each member of the team, listening carefully to their concerns, discussing their agenda, the effectiveness of their own team, whether any personnel changes were needed, and whether they were meeting their goals.

Under extreme time pressure to make the vaccine deadline, Bancel created clear goals and pressed his team to keep an eagle eye on them. For example, in late January 2020, the CEO had a conversation with Juan Andres, his head of manufacturing. Bancel recalls what he describes as "a surreal conversation" where he said to Andres, "I need you to tell me how we're going to make a billion doses next year." Andres gave his CEO a funny look and asked him if he was smoking something: "Dude, there is no way we can make a billion doses next year." Bancel told him that was the wrong answer. "What I really mean is: Tell me what you need to make a billion doses next year." And Andres did. Here the CEO made sure his top team members were aligned with the company's goals and then pushed them to be innovative—and renewed their energy—by expressing confidence in them and giving the tools they needed to succeed.

Bancel explains the trick to strong team dynamics: "Being even more clear than usual on goals, articulating those early, and having the twice-a-week meeting was very useful. But it's also important for the team to keep all the pieces juggling in the air at the same time and not have a big disconnect within the team. The way it should work is that when I'm not in a room, and a subset of them have to accomplish a task together or get aligned on something together, they should have enough pieces of the puzzle that the whole team is aligned and can be effective together."

The big, risky signature move you have in mind might be just what's needed to secure your organization's future, but it will not succeed if you can't get others to back your plan. Leaders often struggle with how to achieve buy-in from their board and executive team. Too often they forge ahead, and when obstacles or delays occur—which are inevitable while executing any big move—they find themselves on their own. Suddenly there's a lot of second-guessing from directors and team members, and in extreme cases opposition can grow and even derail the plan.

When Peter Kelly, the CEO of OPENLANE (formerly KAR Global), decided that his auto auction company would benefit from a radical transformation, he spent a considerable amount of time and effort discussing the major initiative with his board and members of his executive team. To Kelly, it was quite clear when he took on the CEO role in 2021 that he had to accelerate his company into the digital age. This Indiana company with $2.3 billion in annual revenue and ten thousand employees was a leader in the wholesale car auction business. Every year close to ten million vehicles get auctioned in North America. Some of them are coming off a lease, others are being sold by car dealers who can't move them off their lots, and others still are being sold by car rental companies and other commercial fleet owners. For decades the company had held auctions at approximately seventy physical locations in North America where dealers and fleet owners would transport the cars to a site and buyers would gather to bid on them, with the winners hauling them away.

Kelly believed that these physical auctions were becoming too time-consuming and costly for his customers—all that travel and hauling of cars added up—and that in the long run a digitally enabled market platform for sellers and buyers was the answer. Moreover, physical auctions also limited the number of buyers who might be interested in purchasing used cars to those who showed up at the site, whereas a digital auction would open up a much larger market. In fact, Kelly's history in the industry had started when he cofounded a digital auction business, OPENLANE, in 1999 with a view to disrupting the used car auction industry and moving these transactions online. After being independent for twelve years, the company was acquired by KAR Global in 2011, which changed its name to OPENLANE in 2023.

Following its acquisition of OPENLANE, the company continued to build sophisticated software to inspect vehicles, determine a used vehicle's value, and then allow customers to bid for them online. Adoption continued, but it often wasn't as fast as Kelly had hoped—a significant part of the industry still gravitated toward physical auctions.

After he rose from the president's role to CEO in the midst of the COVID pandemic, Kelly knew it was time to accelerate the company's digital transformation. "When I took on the CEO role in March 2021," he says, "it was clear to me that a big part of the agenda was to continue this transition toward digital, but I wasn't at that time thinking we would divest of all our U.S. physical assets. But over time I realized the difficulty of having a foothold in the legacy business while at the same time transitioning to a digitally based business model, as opposed to being fully committed to the digital transition." Ultimately it became clear to him that the logical move was to sell KAR Global's American physical auction business and accelerate the move to a completely digital business model. He also knew that there was an interested buyer for the auction business—the online used car seller Carvana. Kelly recognized that selling the physical auction business would help his company pay down its sizable debt load and put the focus clearly on the new digital model. After the divestiture Kelly would be leading a smaller company in terms of volume, revenue, and head count, but one with a clearer and more focused strategy and underlying investment thesis. He believed that was the right trade-off.

It was a challenging time to undergo a massive transformation. The supply chain disruptions caused by COVID had slowed the production of new cars, causing the supply of used vehicles to decline and their value to appreciate. More expensive and scarce used cars had slowed the wholesale used-vehicle business considerably during the pandemic. Even so, Kelly knew that selling off the physical auction business would better position its industry-leading digital marketplaces for accelerated growth. In his view it increased the rationale for the change of the business model, since "challenging times require bold moves, while pursuing promising opportunities."

While he knew what he had in mind would be challenging, he engaged in an active and in-depth discussion with his board of directors and certain members of the management team to get their input and counsel. He also engaged advisers to do a deep analysis of the fundamentals. Internally, there were many questions and some responsible pushback. The physical auction was both the genesis and the legacy of the company. Some worried that selling the physical auction business would make the company a lot smaller. Others believed the industry challenges impacting physical auctions were temporary and the business would come back. People saw the benefits of a digital future but were also daunted by what executing the move actually meant—divesting close to half of the company's revenue and half of its employees. Kelly continued to believe in his vision for the company, and ultimately his humility, his willingness to admit that there would be challenges, and the fact that he welcomed feedback helped him prevail. He pulled off a tough balancing act by providing vision and direction while at the same time inviting vigorous debate with his management team and board. In 2022 the company successfully sold its physical auction business in the United States to Carvana and committed to an all-digital future.

It's one thing to win the support of your board and executive team when making a bold move, but how do you energize your entire organization to back and execute your plan? That's exactly the challenge that Nissan CEO Makoto Uchida faces as he prepares the global car company that he leads for the transition to electric vehicles. The Japanese automaker has been producing vehicles for more than ninety years, and today operates in all major markets around the world. In 2010, it was the first company to produce a mass-market EV with its innovative Leaf model. More than a decade later, however, Nissan remains primarily a producer of gasoline-powered vehicles, and Uchida knows this has to change.

The world is moving toward EVs, and it is imperative for the traditional automakers to transition quickly, or they might find themselves at a severe competitive disadvantage. Consider that in China, the world's largest car market, new energy vehicles—a category consisting of mostly

EVs—account for roughly one-third of thirty million units sold annually. If Nissan is to remain competitive in China and other major markets, it must innovate in ways that produce more value for consumers, helping Nissan's vehicles to stack up better against market leaders Tesla and BYD in price and features. In addition, it must do all this while achieving strong margins and ROI.

The dilemma, as Uchida sees it, is that Tesla and other EV makers were built from the ground up. They are vertically integrated, controlling critical components of their supply chains. They develop and manufacture many of their own batteries and electric powertrain components, as well as most of their software for various vehicle applications. Also, their manufacturing technologies are done in house. This gives them a competitive advantage over traditional automakers in speed and cost.

By contrast, Nissan and other traditional automakers are horizontally integrated, where they work closely with a huge and sophisticated set of tiered suppliers in a global supply chain. While this has served them well for decades, to compete with the new generation of leaner, faster, and more agile EV makers, they need to challenge some legacy practices while leveraging the inherent strengths of horizontal integration. "How do you change the culture of a legacy company like Nissan, which has been operating as a traditional automotive company for ninety years," says Uchida, "so we can compete against this new era of giant, vertically integrated companies like BYD and Tesla? That's the key question that I am facing."

Nissan has a strong history of innovation, but as with any large company with a long and successful history, complacency can start to creep into the culture. "We have around 130,000 people in our company, and we have a legacy mindset where we believe we have great technology, and to a certain extent that is true," says Uchida. "But we have to change the way we operate to become more competitive in this new world. We need to build agility in our system and maximize diverse opportunities. The challenge is that people become comfortable with the way they do things, and it is very, very difficult to get them out of this comfort zone." In addition, Nissan has historically been a more top-down-driven culture when it comes to generating initiatives and innovation—another hurdle that Uchida needs to address.

The key is to change the mindset of people and transform the culture. To get his organization focused on this transformation, Uchida redefined Nissan's corporate purpose to inspire and motivate employees. In 2021 the company embarked on a transformation plan: the Nissan Ambition 2030 vision. The goal is to become carbon efficient by shifting more of its product and production mix to EVs and autonomous vehicles, creating new sustainable mobility services, and applying circular-economy techniques to Nissan's manufacturing processes. And the company needs to make this transition while enhancing profitability along the way, an enormous task and challenge. Setting a stretch goal is one thing, but getting 130,000 employees to change their operating models and processes in order to achieve those targets is something else entirely.

Uchida realized that he first had to change himself before asking others to do so. That meant finding a balance between being a strong leader who knew what needed to be done and one who could step back and let his people take initiatives and make risky bets. "A leader," says Uchida, "has to be willing to trust people and let them fail, if necessary. You have to lead by the heart and not just by the head."

He continues, "This is hard to do in a culture where people are used to strong leaders. If I reject ideas, if I don't delegate authority, my people will start to think that I don't trust them. The attitude then becomes, 'Why should I keep pushing myself to go beyond what's asked? Why should I challenge myself beyond what's necessary to get by? After all, I have my family, and my life is good, so why should I change the way I work?'"

Finding that balance between leading with both the heart and the mind, being able to provide clear directions while also letting go and inviting his people to take the initiative and be innovative, was a new balancing act, which he learned and practiced at the Bower Forum program.

The first thing Uchida did in his company-wide cultural transformation was to change the configuration of Nissan's executive committee, because he believed this group set the tenor of behavior for the levels of management below them—all the way down to the frontline supervisors. For decades, Nissan headquarters had steered the company.

To decentralize the organization and make it more agile, Uchida invited the company's regional market leaders—including the heads of the United States, China, Mexico, Africa, and Europe—plus the head of product planning to sit on the executive committee. "If you look at the world today, each market is being disrupted. There is fragmentation everywhere. Speed is essential, and what customers want in each market is different, so it made sense to delegate more authority to the regions, while ensuring the right level of standardization in the company's products, platforms, and designs. To have this one team with a new spirit and a more entrepreneurial business style sends a powerful message throughout the organization."

Uchida believes in personally spreading this message of innovation, initiative, risk-taking, and speed, and one of the ways he does this is by holding a seemingly endless series of enterprise-wide roundtables across organizational layers, functions, and regions. He wants the word to spread to the three hundred or so senior managers below the executive committee and to the company's several thousand frontline managers. The idea is for the CEO to set a new tone for change and let it percolate through each layer of management. He wants to show that Nissan is a place where people can be trusted to take risks and where managers encourage their employees to give 100 percent.

One of the big topics of his roundtables is how to get employees to feel safe enough to challenge their team leaders and ask questions. "You have to show that you're a human being, and work is about asking questions human to human," says Uchida. In Nissan's past, whenever one of its CEOs visited a factory, he would be given five prepared questions to answer while all the supervisors and workers stood around and quietly listened to him recite the answers. Today when Uchida visits a factory, he doesn't look at the prepared questions. Instead, he says to the gathered crowd, "Please, I'm human. I'm here. I want to change the company to one where everybody feels proud working here. You can ask any question. And honestly, if I don't know the answer, I'll tell you. So please be free to ask anything." He says he always tries to encourage his employees to say something "from their heart."

By creating a more open and human environment, Uchida's ultimate goal is to get people at all levels of the organization to feel comfortable enough to challenge the old ways of doing things. In previous decades, for example, Nissan had adopted a slew of quality control processes. Uchida asked his people to challenge those processes, without compromising quality results. He wants them to ask: When is the last time someone has analyzed it carefully? Does it still make sense to do it? Does it add value to the customer? Is there a better, faster, and cheaper way to get the same result?

This different kind of mindset is hard to achieve because at Nissan typically a team leader will make a suggestion, and their colleagues might only understand 70 percent of what's being asked but won't seek clarification because they're not inclined to challenge the boss. Now Uchida is inculcating a culture that recognizes that a job can't be done right unless the team member understands 100 percent of what's being discussed, and that can only happen if there's a frank and open discussion. This is a message that the CEO hammers on relentlessly in his roundtables. He says that now people tell him, "But you keep saying the same thing," and that's exactly the response the CEO wants. He quips, "My goal is to sound like a broken record."

How does Uchida know whether his cultural transformation is working? In their annual reviews his managers now get evaluated on teamwork, communication, innovation, and taking the initiative. His HR department conducts a series of surveys to gauge how employees regard their team leaders, whether there's transparency, whether they're encouraged to innovate and take risks. Uchida says the surveys show that Nissan has made good progress in its cultural transformation but that it is a multiyear endeavor, so he keeps pushing forward.

"One of the most valuable things another CEO told me," he says, "is that employees don't remember what you said or what you achieved, but they do remember how you made them *feel*. You have to appeal to their hearts. You have to make them want to do something great together. That to me is the definition of leadership."

Uchida started practicing leading with his heart and mind first for himself and now is applying that approach to his entire organization.

Questions to help you engage your team and give them the courage and resolve to make bold moves:

///

- Do I have a team that can face upcoming challenges or merely the team that has gotten us where we are?

- Am I asking leaders questions that help them achieve a bold move rather than ones that ask whether it is possible?

- Do we share a sense of camaraderie and excitement about what is possible?

- Am I clear on what's required to win, on my expectations for the team, and on what the team can expect of me?

- Is bold leadership an important part of assessing performance?

///

In Summary

///

G reat leaders recognize which bold move shows the most promise, garner the courage to make the move, and then find ways to get the rest of the organization to understand and enthusiastically buy into the new strategy or initiative. As we've seen in the examples above, this requires that you make the strategy and purpose of the organization crystal clear while at the same time helping your teams renew their energy and enthusiasm. It also takes understanding what motivates every member and learning how to interact with each in a way that brings out the best in them.

Once people are aligned, the best leaders know that it's now time to give them the space to perform at their highest level.

9

CONTROL IS AN ILLUSION

A t one Bower Forum in New York City, a CEO of a global manufacturer bemoaned the fact that everything seemed to be spinning out of control. Cyberattacks were running rampant, the pandemic and the war in Ukraine were disrupting supply chains, and inflation was hurting the bottom line. "I feel like I'm spending more time dealing with these externalities than with the business," he said. "It's become a huge distraction for both me and my managers." Another CEO sitting at the table tried to add some perspective. She said, "Look, you can't control politics, you can't control wars happening around the world, and you can't control where interest rates are heading. But what you can control is how you act in a time of disruption and uncertainty. If you can't control how higher interest rates or supply chain shortages are hurting your business, you can control the way you talk about your value proposition, about how your products can increase productivity and efficiency, you can talk about how you're investing capital for when the trouble subsides. Get your team focused on those things that only you can do—improving your business in tough times."

Like our manufacturing CEO, you have probably spent your career thinking that you're in control. You worked hard and did well in school, and then at work you followed the rules and rose steadily up the ladder. You knew what you needed to do and did it, and you were rewarded for your efforts. Something happens, however, the higher you climb in an organization. Suddenly you're responsible for more and more people and their performance. You can't do all their jobs—although, control freak that you are, you would like to—yet you are responsible for the success of the organization.

The days when an imperial CEO stood astride an organization are over. Today, the best leaders realize that control is an illusion. In our ninth leadership element, "Empower People," we ask you to define what it is that only *you* can do, given that you can't do everything. Ask yourself, "What are my priorities?" Maybe it's formulating a new strategy, or overseeing a technological transformation, or clarifying your mandate from the board. Or maybe it's all three. Once you have decided what it is that only you can do, you then set the direction and stand out of the way. This means asking the questions that make people think, as opposed to telling them what to do. You can explain what your own experience has been, but the answer has to come from within the other person.

Letting go inevitably means that some people in your organization will go off in the wrong direction. You need to have the patience to let them learn from their mistakes. During Super Bowl LVII, Philadelphia Eagles quarterback Jalen Hurts fumbled late in the game, contributing to his team's loss. Rather than feeling self-pity, he looked at it as a learning experience. After the matchup he said, "You either win or you learn. Win, lose, I always reflect on the things I could have done better, anything you could have done better to try and take that next step."

The key then is to find the right balance between control and letting people have agency and the freedom to make mistakes—as long as they learn from them and don't repeat them. Rob Painter, a Bower Forum attendee, is the CEO of Trimble, a global technology firm that supplies cutting-edge software and hardware to the agriculture, construction, geospatial, and transportation industries. He says that rather than fight for control, leaders should embrace individuality and the need for everyone to have at least some freedom to express themselves and implement their ideas. "The notion," says Painter, "is that we embrace individuality, but we win together." At one leadership program Painter was conducting at his company, he noticed the wide mix of functions represented in the room. He asked the group to put themselves in one another's shoes: "How many of you have ever written a line of code, how many of you know how a journal entry works, how many of you have ever created a marketing requirements document, and how many of you have asked for a sales order and know what that feels like to get turned down?"

No one, not even the CEO, knows how to do all these jobs, yet to let all these different players act on their own can lead to chaos. Painter's answer is to look at a business like a symphony where all the players come together to make beautiful music. "This can be," he says, "both wildly comforting and extraordinarily uncomfortable at the same time. Because CEOs can see more of the organization than anyone else, they take on the role of an orchestra conductor. I don't know how to play all the instruments, but I can create an environment where I can fine-tune the orchestra. I can help everyone understand what to focus on—what piece we should be playing, are we playing it too slowly or are some of the players out of tune, and if so, what do we need to do to fix it?"

So, for a leader, the key issue is not so much how you can gain control but what are the things that only *you* can do? What things do you need to control, and what should you release for others to lead? That's another way of saying, what are the areas where you can have the most impact? "There's a whole set of tasks I could work on that are totally gratifying," says Painter, "but as CEO, I'm not positioned to move the needle on those things."

Some jobs only the CEO can do because of their personal skills, or because the work cuts across multiple parts of the organization, or because it has a disproportionate impact on the organization.

With that in mind, you have to ask yourself, what are your top two or three priorities, the things that only you can do that will make a difference? At Trimble, Painter's first priority is establishing how the business is going to win. His second is to get a clear strategic mandate from the board—something he certainly can't delegate. And third is to make sure the company's technological transformation is on track. "These are the three things I believe I can uniquely do and where I devote the most time setting the tone," says Painter. In a practical sense, that means defining success and putting the right people in the right orchestra seats. By framing his job in this way, Painter doesn't have complete control, but he has a certain amount by being able to intercede where he sees a problem.

Painter works hard to make sure his managers think the same way about control. Historically, Trimble had been a very decentralized business, with its construction, agricultural, and transportation divisions basically running their own fiefdoms. Wanting Trimble to become more of a matrix organization, Painter decided to create a corporate technology team to achieve efficiencies of scale and give his IT people more freedom. It was a hard sell to the heads of each business unit. "I tried," says Painter, "to get my managers to understand that they don't have to own or control all the resources. So we'd have these 'control is an illusion' conversations where I'd tell them, 'Yes, you do have all these cyber resources reporting to you, but do you really have any idea what they

are doing, and do you really have any ability to add value to them?'"
Today, Trimble has put all its cyber experts together in one organization
to act as a shared service in which employees have career paths, more
autonomy, and can perform more efficiently. Control, in this case, had
been costly.

A s we've seen so far in this chapter, the best leaders grant authority
and then try to minimize mistakes by creating a modicum of control
and by keeping people from straying too far from the company's goals
and values. On a day-to-day basis, that's a hard act to pull off. The best
CEOs use different metrics for monitoring and enforcing that balance
between control and autonomy. The challenge here is to create an environment that provides both psychological safety and accountability. This
is another polarity that leaders must master. On the one hand, a safe environment can't come at the cost of accountability. This can lead to a culture of complacency where tough conversations are avoided and highly
motivated people become demoralized. On the other hand, a safe environment can't be sacrificed on the altar of accountability. This can lead
to a fear-based culture.

One leader who balanced a safe environment with accountability is
Frank D'Souza, the former CEO and cofounder of the global technology services firm Cognizant and cofounder and managing partner of
Recognize, a technology investment platform. Cognizant helps corporations modernize technology, reimagine processes, and transform experiences so they can stay at the forefront of our fast-changing world.
D'Souza became CEO of Cognizant in 2007 and grew the then $1.4 bil-
lion per year revenue company more than tenfold; when he stepped down
in 2019, the company was bringing in over $16 billion per year. Cognizant
appeared on *Fortune* magazine's "100 Fastest-Growing Companies" list

for eleven consecutive years. He attributes much of his success to a system that he says helps build strong, purpose-driven, and independent leaders who consistently operate at peak performance.

When D'Souza took over as CEO, he faced a problem that many business leaders would love to have: His company was on a rapid growth trajectory. Yet he knew that if he didn't attain a certain size and scale, his IT firm was going to get stuck in the middle of the pack with a market position that was too big to be as nimble as a small company but not big enough to compete in the major leagues. Growing Cognizant to scale was of the essence. His core constraint, however, was not capital—it was leadership. D'Souza believed he needed to grow leaders at least 20 percent faster than the growth rate of the company; if Cognizant was growing by 50 percent annually, he would need to develop 70 percent more leaders than he had the year before.

D'Souza recognized that the growth he was striving for would require him to take significant risks and make bold decisions that would prove make-or-break moments for his tenure as CEO. "My philosophy is we rent these jobs; we don't own them," he says. "We're in these jobs for a very short period of time, so every day you've got to earn the right to be in that chair, and if you're not earning the right to be in that chair then you shouldn't be in that chair, and if there's somebody better than you, you should step down. My stewardship of the company and my fiduciary obligation to all my shareholders and my other stakeholders is to maximize the value of the company, not to do what's best for Frank."

To the challenge of growing high-quality leaders so rapidly, D'Souza applied an engineering mindset. First, when hiring, he searched for people who were both highly capable and intrinsically motivated. "As a young CEO," he recalls, "I had this deep-seated fear that I didn't know enough to do the job, so I found and surrounded myself with extraordinarily qualified people who were smarter than I was. That was the only way that I could learn and grow. But capability was not enough; I also wanted people who took initiative and navigated novel and complex situations without my direct involvement. I had read a lot about intrinsic motivation by researchers and writers like Edward Deci, Daniel Pink, and Jim Collins. Intrinsically motivated people want autonomy, they want a sense of mastery, and they want to feel purpose. Developing intrinsically motivated leaders who were highly capable became the core of our leadership development approach."

To help his leaders succeed, D'Souza created an environment in which Cognizant managers were encouraged to pursue autonomy, mastery, and purpose, and then he stepped aside to let them do what they needed to support the company's objectives. "It was a culture of high psychological safety," he says, "where people felt comfortable working on their own and doing their own thing." He gave them the freedom to hone their skills and become the best in their class at what they did.

Next, he combined deep empowerment with a rigorous performance management process so that he could identify where leaders were doing well, in addition to where they were falling short. The idea was that D'Souza could maintain their sense of autonomy, but, when necessary, intervene and try to help them grow. "Our core philosophy was that we wanted to serve a small number of clients and we wanted to serve them very deeply," he says. "Everybody says that, but we tried very hard to live up to that ideal in everything we did. That meant that we had to keep decision making very close to the client. We couldn't be top-down and bureaucratic. Issues couldn't come all the way up to headquarters every time a decision had to be made."

To keep his leaders close to Cognizant's customers, D'Souza made sure they had the resources they needed. He also created tools to monitor their performance. He installed a leadership dashboard consisting of four basic metrics meant to keep his leaders on track: revenue, profitability, employee satisfaction, and customer satisfaction. D'Souza viewed these metrics as guardrails that would keep his intrinsically motivated leaders on track and in line with the company's goals and values. Success at Cognizant meant balancing all four metrics. Making your numbers wasn't enough if your customers were unhappy. Yet happy customers were not enough if your employees were miserable, which probably meant you were burning out your teams. "In the early days, when we had to hire leaders from the outside, many of them prioritized some subset of these metrics," says D'Souza. "Some new hires had come from highly competitive, scorched-earth companies where they learned to deliver the numbers at all costs. Unsurprisingly, they had trouble bringing their teams along and satisfying our customers. By tracking all four metrics, we could intervene and help them change their behavior."

D'Souza also looked for symbolic ways to spread the message that success at Cognizant was about more than making the numbers. In order to highlight the importance of customer satisfaction, he would stage gatherings with three thousand or more employees to celebrate and award those who did the most for their clients. Every year, he would also invite a group of eight to ten of Cognizant's top customers to attend a strategy session with the board of directors and share what it was like working with Cognizant—both the good and the bad. "The ritual of having customers show up at the board," says D'Souza, "sent a powerful message throughout the organization that the board took seriously how we treated our customers." Through newsletters and blogs, Cognizant would send to the entire organization summaries of what the customers told the board. The message was, yes, you had to deliver your financial targets, but you couldn't do it at the expense of the customer. "The customer," says D'Souza, "became our true north."

This approach to building leaders did more than just make Cognizant a major player in its industry and a financial success. The impact and success of D'Souza's methods were seen beyond the walls of his company. Since his departure from Cognizant, at least fourteen of his top executives have moved on to become CEOs at other companies.

Maintaining the balance between control and freedom is particularly challenging in the nonprofit world, where a dashboard like the one D'Souza created, containing profit and loss metrics, isn't possible. At the nonprofit Teach for All, a global network of national organizations that place motivated university graduates as teachers at schools in underprivileged communities and develop their leadership skills, founder Wendy Kopp created her own north star, which she calls collective leadership.

While a student of public policy at Princeton University's Princeton School of Public and International Affairs, Kopp had a eureka moment after she saw first-generation college students struggle with academics while her classmates who had attended top prep schools breezed through the curriculum. The inequality of the American education system so impressed her that she wrote her thesis on the need for a national service corps for teachers. The notion was to persuade bright young grads from all academic majors to commit two years to teach in schools in low-income areas. After graduating, Kopp in 1990 raised $2.5 million from corporate sponsors and philanthropists to launch Teach for America. Before long, Teach for America became a must-do stop for many graduates of the country's top universities. By 2022 the organization had placed some seventy thousand teachers in America's public schools. The idea was not only to help these underserved schools by bringing in bright young teachers, many of whom had much-needed STEM skills, but also to create a generation of leaders who better understood the challenges facing marginalized students and could help influence change as they continued working as educators, social innovators, politicians, policy experts, business executives, and journalists.

During the early days of Teach for America, Kopp worked endless hours traveling to universities to recruit students and also to underserved schools around the country to sell them on the new program. She spent time creating an organization comprised of local offices charged with maximizing impact in their communities but still centrally managed.

The first international adaptation of Teach for America was Teach First in the United Kingdom, launched in 2002. By 2007, Kopp found herself fielding an increasing number of requests from individuals around the world who wanted to see their countries benefit from initiatives like Teach for America and were looking for help. Kopp wanted to respond to these requests but was overwhelmed just thinking about the challenge. She knew what went into launching and scaling Teach for America and couldn't imagine how to do something similar on a global scale. Ultimately, she worked with the founder of Teach First to develop a plan for launching Teach for All, a global network of independent, locally led organizations tied to a global organization that would accelerate progress by helping everyone learn from one another.

The night before former president Bill Clinton and British prime minister Tony Blair were to announce the launch of Teach for All at the September 2007 Clinton Global Initiative, Kopp panicked. "I thought to myself, 'How is this going to work? We scaled Teach for America through obsessive attention to detail and tremendous attention to building strong management systems. How will we possibly have a similar level of impact in such a loose, far-flung network?'"

One of her work partners assured her that it would be okay: "There's no turning back—they will announce this tomorrow, and we'll just evolve from there." Today, the global network includes national organizations in more than sixty countries on six continents that are striving to achieve educational equity and excellence for all of their nations' children.

A large part of Kopp's success with Teach for All was her willingness to give up control and trust partners around the world with ownership and full responsibility for their organizations' success. She embraced this strategy in part because she reflected on how important this was for her own success as a social entrepreneur in the United States. Also, she felt it was important given that the very purpose of the network was to develop strong leaders who could help all children fulfill their potential.

To make this approach work, Teach for All established a clear set of unifying core principles and then created a culture where leaders constantly learn from one another and take those learnings and apply them where applicable in their own countries. What other organizations put into management and control, Teach for All invests in facilitating learning and offering leadership development. Says Kopp, "This is hard and messy work, and there will be challenges, but what I've seen is that this network approach fosters more rapid continuous improvement."

The unifying principles that Kopp created started with commitment to a shared purpose, to a theory of change, a vision, and values defining how network participants will engage with each other globally. The global leadership team of Teach for All shares best practices with the local teams to help them make the best possible decisions for their particular countries. "We wanted all our network partners," says Kopp, "to learn from those who came before them, but also to be able to innovate and adapt that which made the most sense in their own countries. There's such power in fostering grassroots efforts while also helping people gain global exposure."

When building up Teach for All, Kopp, a driven social entrepreneur, had to keep reminding herself that control is indeed an illusion. She had to step back and respect the local leaders who wanted to design their own approaches within the Teach for All framework that reflected their cultural needs and economic situations. "It's a hard line to figure out when to jump in," she says, "because it's important to let local leaders chart their own course, but it also doesn't make sense to let each country keep making the same mistakes over and over." For example, unlike in the United States, local governments in India don't pay for teachers—the school system is largely private. Shaheen Mistri, the head of Teach for India, took the initiative and created a fundraising organization to pay for her teachers' salaries, and also worked to instill political change by persuading some local governments to chip in for educational costs. The approached worked, and Teach for India is a thriving organization recognized in India and globally as a success story. It has served as an inspiration for other Teach for All programs facing similar challenges.

To sit back and be comfortable watching organizations make different choices takes a deep belief in others and respect for their judgment. "I really felt for these people who were starting and leading these organizations given that I did it myself and I know how excruciatingly hard it was," says Kopp. "Very quickly, I realized that my initial misgivings at the outset of Teach for All were unfounded as I started seeing people improving on what we had done at Teach for America." The idea was to let innovation flourish and to intercede when core principles were being forgotten.

One important tenet of collective leadership is that learning is a two-way street. Kopp, for example, ended up seeing some ways that Teach for America itself could learn from Teach for India. When Teach for India launched, Kopp flew to the country several times to visit Mistri. Teach for India had embraced much of Teach for America's teacher training curriculum but adapted it for the Indian context. In the United

States, the curriculum focused mostly on developing teacher knowledge and skills, but Mistri evolved it to include training sessions around mind-set development, where teachers learned to appreciate the potential of marginalized students and developed the courage to apply high standards even when confronted with extraordinary challenges. Kopp was impressed by Mistri's teacher training program, and at her urging Teach for America flew dozens of its own trainers to India to see how they did it. "It takes collective leadership to change a system," says Kopp. "We see this across our network, where so many brilliant, committed people, influenced by the diversity of contexts and culture, are innovating and developing strong solutions. We can learn and move much faster by letting them innovate and lead in ways they think make sense."

Teach for All is much more than a mechanism for providing good teachers to local schools. Most of the graduates who leave teaching after their two years stay involved in education in various ways. Of more than one hundred thousand Teach for All network alumni, 74 percent are still working full time to improve education and related systemic issues. "You can't change the system with one person at the top," says Kopp. "It's going to take collective leadership—diverse people throughout the system exercising agency and leadership toward shared purpose and learning and collaborating together."

Questions to help you balance control and free agency:

//

- What are my top two or three priorities, the things that only I can do that will make a difference? Have I delegated the rest?

- What can we control? What can we not control but influence? What can we neither control nor influence?

- Am I clear about how that translates to who can make which decisions in the organization and how?

- Once I have set a direction for the company, have I given my people the resources they need to succeed and then stepped out of the way to provide sufficient space for them to lead?

- Which questions should I ask to make people think as opposed to telling them what to do?

- How can I explain less about my own experiences, and instead encourage my colleagues to share their views and come up with the answers?

- How do I encourage people from other parts of the business to share best practices in order to avoid repeating mistakes?

//

In Summary

///

The best leaders find the right balance between control and letting people have the agency to take the initiative and inevitably make some mistakes. They know what decisions must be made centrally to drive consistency, and what guiding principles allow everyone to make the right call without the risk of compromising the organization's purpose and values. By doing so, they can focus on only those things they can control. The same goes for each member of your team. You can help your team balance the dichotomy between control and agency by having them ask, "What can we control? What must be consistent across the organization? What can we not control but influence? What can we neither control nor influence? And what are those skills, mindsets, and capabilities that we need to become successful leaders?"

Creating a fine balance between autonomy and control, however, will only work if you know what's really going on inside your organization. Otherwise, how can you intercede when a project or initiative is about to derail?

10

Encourage Truth Telling

EVERYONE KEEPS THINGS FROM THE BOSS

One participant at the Bower Forum who had been CEO for only a year complained that the people in his organization no longer told him what was really going on. Since he became the boss, he no longer had any peers, and those frank conversations he used to have with his colleagues disappeared. He felt lost and worried that some bad news would eventually blindside him.

One of our coaches who had spent years running a Fortune 100 global manufacturing company explained that sometimes you have to look outside of the company to get the truth, but that's not enough. The veteran CEO explained to the young attendee that he should gather his direct reports whether it's for a strategy, budget, or planning meeting and "you have to convince people that they can disagree with you, and that you want them to disagree with you and make sure you engage them in a vigorous debate on the issues. Tell them you're going to learn something from all of them and you respect their opinions as opposed to acting like a king who can't be involved in the conversation anymore."

A year later the young CEO reported back to the Forum, saying that while those kinds of frank conversations with his staff were tough at first, eventually the people in the room became more comfortable raising difficult issues and discussing bad news. The culture of his executive team became more open, and he, as CEO, became perceived as first among equals.

As the coach pointed out in this session, no one wants to be the bearer of unfortunate news, which is why the boss is often the last one to find out what's really going on. Such a reluctance to speak truth to power can have dire consequences for a business. That's because it's foundational that everybody have the same view of the reality. If people in the organization lack a common understanding of the reality of both the internal and external challenges they are facing, it will be very hard to develop the kind of conviction, call to action, and sense of urgency that every successful organization depends upon to execute well. If members of the team don't have all the facts or are afraid to share them, miscues and entropy become inevitable.

The consequences can be dire. In 1961, President John F. Kennedy gave the green light for an invasion of communist Cuba at the Bay of Pigs. The Cuban exile force that the U.S. government had trained and equipped for the invasion was ill prepared, and the operation turned into a fiasco, with the Cuban government quickly crushing the invasion. Kennedy's advisers, it later turned out, had not fully informed the president about the potential risks and challenges of the operation. If Kennedy had had the full picture, he might have avoided this tragedy. Historians have debated why his advisers didn't speak candidly about the risks—why they didn't warn him that the Cuban exile force was ill prepared and why they downplayed the likely strong response from Fidel Castro's government. Some argue that Kennedy's advisers might have been hesitant to share bad news with the president for fear of appearing disloyal or being seen as undermining the mission. Others believe that a culture of groupthink or conformity within the administration discouraged dissenting views or alternative perspectives. Whichever the case, the failure of Kennedy's advisers to fully inform the president of the risks led to a disastrous mission that left a lasting mark on his legacy.

Conversely, building a culture where openness is the norm can pay big benefits. A notable example of this happened at Ford Motor in 2006, when Alan Mulally, a top executive at Boeing, was brought in to get the money-losing automaker back on track. Mulally developed a system where at his staff meetings, executives would mark a project green if it was on track and red if there were problems. At a meeting early in his tenure, all the projects got a green flag. Incredulous, Mulally challenged the executives, asking how all the projects could be going well if the company was losing money. Finally, one brave soul changed his color to red, which broke the ice and led to a frank discussion of all of Ford's problems and, a few years later, an eventual turnaround.

To get the scoop about what's happening, leaders have to dig deep into the organization. It's important to be approachable, to have an open-door policy, but that's not enough. As we saw in the example at Ford, most people simply won't tell the boss what's going on for fear of being criticized or penalized. In our tenth leadership element, "Encourage Truth Telling," we suggest that leaders build their own inner circles of advisers and then leverage them by listening to them carefully. This goes for not only the CEO but more broadly for leaders throughout the organization. One way to jump-start the process is by creating informal networks of "truth tellers" who keep you grounded in reality. These informal networks work across functions, regions, business lines, and layers of the organization. When working well, they can provide valuable feedback on the future direction of the company through a frank exchange of ideas.

While many leaders say they welcome dissent, when their team members actually push back, they can be defensive or feel insecure about the decision making. One approach that helps is what we call "contributory dissent." The goal is to turn conflict into creative debates by encouraging teams to air their differences in a way that expands perspectives and invites healthy opposition. As a result, decision making and complex problem solving gets faster and smarter.

McKinsey's research and experience in the field point to several steps leaders can take to engage in healthy dissent:

Lead to inspire, not to direct:

- Empower the group to come up with ideas: "None of us knows the answer yet, but we can work it out together if we harness the best of everyone's thinking."

Foster dissent by actively seeking it:

- Explicitly seek diverse views; give people permission and encouragement.
- Consider including dissent as a stated organizational value.
- Make provisions for open and unconstrained discussion in the buildup to decisions.

Welcome open discussion when it comes:

- Listen to dissenters and naysayers and thank them for their insights.

- Recognize dissent as a usefully unfiltered channel for understanding the organization's perceptions on issues.
- Invite dissenters to become part of the decision-making process so they become positive influencers later during implementation.
- Employ deliberate techniques such as pre-mortems to widen the debate and mitigate groupthink.

The overall goal is to get people to speak truth to power, a rare occurrence in most organizations, where office politics reign. People have sharp antennas and quickly pick up signals in meetings. It's the job of a leader to constantly reinforce the notion that they are not the smartest ones in the room and that they not only want but also demand healthy dialogue and constructive disagreement. Jim Owens, who ran the heavy equipment manufacturer Caterpillar from 2004 to 2010, and who today is a Bower Forum coach, has his own formula for getting people to challenge his ideas.

In his early days of running Caterpillar, Owens soon realized this global behemoth was adrift. The company had fifteen corporate objectives—many of them worthy endeavors—but the executive team didn't really have a clear sense of direction. Nor did the company have strong buy-in from the management ranks on what the business should be. Wishing to give his large organization some traction by helping everyone understand where the business was headed, Owens made a controversial move. He formed a strategic planning committee and purposefully left out many of his direct reports. He asked all of the group presidents who reported to him to nominate those they thought were the smartest people in the company. Owens asked for a combination of global managers from engineering, manufacturing, and marketing. He wanted the company's best strategic thinkers. In the end, the committee consisted of fifteen people, and they met on a Friday or Saturday once a month for a year. At the end of the year, the group published its vision and road map, then worked to get corporate buy-in for a plan that would drive the ship in a vigorous direction for the next five to six years.

"I remember one of the very early meetings," says Owens. "I said, 'One of the things that we all have to come to grips with is that I'm not the smartest guy in the room. Most of you know a whole lot more about areas of this company than I do. I expect vigorous debate and I expect you to disagree with me when you can, and if you don't feel comfortable doing that, you shouldn't be on the committee.'" At the meeting, there were a few managers who knew Owens well and took him at his word. When the others saw that these managers were challenging Owens, they eventually joined in the fracas. At the same time, Owens kept his group presidents whom he had not invited to the meetings up to date so they would be comfortable with the committee's ideas when they were finally published. "If you want to hear the truth," says Owens, "you've got to really lay yourself out there and express a willingness for people to disagree with you, because it's suboptimal if you don't get those best ideas from everyone."

Two major initiatives came out of the committee. One was that Caterpillar should focus on becoming a leader in Asia, especially in India and China. That didn't mean the company would ignore its business in North America, Europe, and South America, but the emphasis would be on winning in Asia, where much of the growth in demand for construction equipment would be. The second initiative was to have every one of its twenty-eight divisions do annual financial stress tests to make sure that the company could weather a severe economic downturn and make money even in the worst-case scenario. Historically Caterpillar suffered from a boom or bust cycle. When the U.S. economy tanked, so did Caterpillar. During the recession of the early 1980s, the company was losing a million dollars a day for three straight years and nearly went bankrupt.

Both strategies served Caterpillar well. With the new focus on Asia, top-line growth soared because all the teams were pulling in the same direction. The annual stress test was not popular with all managers. From 2004 to 2008, the company was growing nicely, and many thought that the stress test was a waste of their time and resources. Then, in 2008, the head of one of the largest global mining companies told Caterpillar that he would buy all the equipment it could make. But later that year the financial crisis hit, and in 2009 Caterpillar saw its revenue drop dramatically. But because the divisions had planned for years for such an event, the company was able to move quickly and lay off forty-six thousand people in the first quarter of 2009, while staying profitable. When the economy started to recover, Caterpillar rehired most of those people, and the business recovered quickly. In 2009, the company's share price was trading at around $22. By 2011, it was back to an all-time high of $120. By encouraging his people to speak truth to power, Owens formulated a dual strategy that kept the once volatile company prospering for nearly a decade.

Some CEOs take a more subtle approach when trying to get their team to speak truth to power. Peter, a CEO of a New York–based media giant, faced a daunting challenge that he shared at the Bower Forum—how to keep the dialogue flowing in a culture notorious for secrecy, backstabbing, personal alliances, and cutthroat competition. Peter oversaw a collection of independent fiefdoms run by headstrong managers. "You can imagine what happens," he says, "when you take a group of high achievers who consider themselves to be very creative and definitely the 'smartest people' in the room and put them in a structure which empowers independence of thinking and information hoarding. No one wanted to talk about what was going on. It was a culture where people disguised things and bent the truth." Sometimes to get their way, a manager would simply say, "The president said this is what he wants," even if they hadn't talked to him. After one executive retired, she said the best thing about retirement was she no longer had to walk down the halls and when someone said good morning have to think about what they really meant.

To get a strong grasp on what was going on in a culture steeped in secrecy, Peter created an informal listening network. "You're kidding yourself," he says, "if you think you know what's going on by taking a factory tour or giving a town hall and once you answer a few questions, which might be filtered or planted by someone in the organization, you then fly off to your next spot. You need people who can tell you what's really going on." To do so, he reached out to employees at all levels of the organization.

Peter would take some out to lunch. With others he played pickup basketball. With others still, he would make it a point when passing them in the hall to stop, listen, and really care about what was going on in their lives. They didn't become friends, but this gesture made employees feel like they could talk with him about a variety of things. His human intelligence network let him know what was really going on: Someone in the organization might be going through a really hard time—they might be suffering through a divorce, their spouse might have cancer, or a child might be severely ill. Or two people in the executive team might not be getting along. "If you don't know that," he said, "you're not able to reach out and provide some proactive support."

"My goal," said Peter, "was to make my sources feel safe enough and assure them of confidentiality so they could talk about anything. I didn't pry but I tried to make my queries part of a natural conversation about how things are going, how are you getting along with this or that manager. This was helpful because if I went through normal channels, the information would get filtered at every stage up through the organization and end up basically becoming the party line."

Among Peter's sources were a manager of the production department, the deputy head of publicity, and many salespeople who had access to many corners of the organization. Some of his most valuable sources were his executive assistants. The assistants talked to other executive assistants and learned what was going on elsewhere in the organization. But to get them to share what was sometimes delicate information, the CEO cultivated meaningful relationships. "You need to let people see that you really care about them. I'd often ask how she was doing and how things were at home. We'd talk a bit and after a while the floodgates would open, and she'd say, 'You won't believe what's going on over in the sales division.'"

Peter was careful never to use any intelligence for punitive purposes. The exercise made him more attuned to different perspectives and reminded him to never forget the human on the other end of any decision.

I f a team isn't performing well, it might be because some of its members feel uncomfortable, neglected, or disrespected. In chapter 4, we discussed how leaders need to identify their own triggers and make sure these emotional cues don't lead to negative behavior. In the same way, leaders have to make sure that members of their team can do the same—recognize their triggers and manage them in a way that mitigates negative behavior.

In a team environment, what one member says or does can trigger a deeply rooted emotional reaction in another member, one that threatens their sense of self and what matters to them. One executive we worked with grew up with a deep need to keep the peace. If things weren't going smoothly or if team members were engaging in heated arguments, that would trigger his need for harmony, and he would try to shut down the debate and suggest a safe solution that wasn't necessarily the best one for the business. It was disorienting for the other members of the team because they wanted to grow and to debate new, challenging ideas, but every time they did, he would try to stop the debate. He needed harmony.

Most executive teams struggle to engage in creative dissent and decision making on complex issues such as setting priorities, capital allocations, and managing organizational interdependencies. What makes these issues challenging is rarely the technical and logical problem solving. It is the emotional and identity issues that lead to ineffective human dynamics. During meetings, leaders need to realize that almost everybody at the table is in their own trigger pattern.

Executives can easily get triggered and react from fear. There are predictable patterns. Some will move against the group by interrupting, taking control, pushing harder, and becoming more directive; some will move away by withdrawing, becoming emotionally distant, getting hyper-logical or finding flaws in others' arguments; others still will move toward the group by deferring, agreeing too easily, and avoiding challenging conversations or feedback in the fear of damaging relationships. All of a sudden, the tension rises, and you end up with a group of senior executives who are in their reactive tendencies and are struggling to solve a complex issue. This happens not because of ill intent but because they care, and the stakes feel high. In these moments, it can feel like you're with a bunch of teenagers trying to solve a complex business issue.

These reactive behaviors are driven by fear. The antidote is not to make people feel bad or judge or shame them but to encourage them to be curious. Something—a fear or a need—got triggered. Get the team to acknowledge the tension and ask questions to understand the concern, fear, or worry behind their reactive behavior.

This kind of negative behavior will continue until the team starts having open discussions about everyone's triggers. Until the members understand what words or behaviors will trigger a negative reaction in each individual, the old habits will dominate the chemistry of the group.

At a London financial firm, we had the executive team spend two days doing role-playing games and talking about what triggered them and how they could work around it. After a while, people started to loosen up and have frank discussions about their fears and insecurities. They were talking as human beings, not just as heads of different corporate functions. After the exercise, the general counsel said, "For the first time, I'm really excited to come to work on Monday. We have been working together for years and we seemed to be a real functioning team, and we were super nice to each other, but we really didn't know each other."

Sometimes people are afraid to tell the person at the top what's really going on for fear of getting on their bad side and incurring their anger. The way a leader interacts with colleagues, especially in difficult situations, can have a telling effect on the level of honesty and openness in an organization. The more annoyed or upset a leader acts, the less likely someone who sees that reaction will be willing to share bad news in the future. It's understandable that CEOs sometimes react negatively to bad news. After all, most decisions that leaders make are not the easy ones—those decisions have already been made by someone else in the organization. Because the buck stops at their desk, CEOs get to decide those 51-percent-to-49-percent decisions, the ones that can go either way.

Trimble CEO Rob Painter runs a complicated business—the company uses GPS to survey construction sites, provides automation to farm equipment to maximize yields and minimize fertilizer use, and uses data analytics to optimize shipping logistics—so there are a lot of those 51-percent-to-49-percent decisions to be made. To make sure he knew what was going on in his organization before making a big decision, Painter would talk to employees a level or two below his executive team. "I'm a curious person. I'm not hierarchical, so I don't care about going through layers to get the information I need. I'll wander the halls or the cafeteria talking to employees. I want to know who are the best and brightest or who can teach me something that I'm curious about and who's got a perspective to tell me what's really going on even if the news is bad."

Early in his tenure as CEO, Painter found that when he was in meetings where he had to make a tough decision, he wasn't always getting the unvarnished truth from his colleagues. After some self-reflection, he realized that he was part of the problem. One time in an important meeting, one of his executives had shared some bad news on the numbers, and Painter blurted out, "All you ever do is bring me bad news! I need some good news. Are you here to tell me we have a problem, are you here to solve the problem, or are you here just to delegate it to me?"

About a month later, one of his reports mentioned to Painter how he was afraid to give him some bad news, and the CEO thought to himself, "'Oh no, I've created an environment where people are afraid to tell me the truth.' I realized that what I had said in that meeting was not only wrong but had reverberated throughout the organization. So I apologized. I acknowledged to my team that when I had said that I 'didn't want any bad news,' it was in a moment of weakness and exhaustion, and I told them that I'd like to take those words back, and that you should feel comfortable telling me what's really going on."

After that confession, Painter found that his people started to be more open with him, but it took a long time to regain trust. The words a CEO says can cast a long shadow on every corner of an organization. Now whenever he speaks, Painter chooses his words carefully, trying to set the right tone and not letting his emotions or his exhaustion cause him to say things he regrets. "Now I'm super conscious in any meeting about what I'll say," he says, "because now I know the length of that shadow and how fast and far it spreads."

Another way to build trust and ensure that your team is taking a healthy perspective is to invite the critics, the truth tellers, and those who typically don't speak up to voice their opinions. You can do this by constantly asking, "What might we be missing?" This helps the team spot risks in advance and solve for avoidable mistakes. It helps them learn faster from inevitable failures, or even to create intentional failures through experiments that can de-risk the future. What is key is to approach these failures not to blame and shame but to rapidly learn and bounce forward. As we have learned in many Bower Forum sessions and from our broader client service work, the lessons learned from failures remain an untapped source of deep insights for better future performance.

It's not that hard to open oneself up to people you feel comfortable with and who in many ways seem just like you—who are one of the club. The best leaders know how to get team members from very different backgrounds and who have very different ideas to better understand one another and engage in open conversation. They learn to open themselves to criticism, creating an atmosphere of constructive debate anchored in facts and insights but also transparent about assumptions and prerequisites. Foremost, they create a culture of true trust, which builds on understanding one another's differences, strengths, and weaknesses and the purposeful and good intentions of every key executive.

One way to encourage more openness is by overcoming some deep-seated stereotypes. When Ford's Mark Fields started running the auto-maker's luxury brand group in Europe—which included Aston Martin, Land Rover, Lincoln, and Volvo—executives at the different marques had a history of working poorly together. They had different mentalities and definitions of luxury, making it hard for them to collaborate and achieve cost savings. They rarely cooperated. Fields wanted the different brands to look at their platforms, components, and software systems to see what they could share without damaging the brand identity. Some of the executives were British, some German. They didn't want much to do with one another.

Fields asked the C-suite of each company to meet for a trust-building exercise. Each group had to draw a cartoon of their perceptions of the other groups. The Land Rover people came up with a drawing of a Jaguar executive with a martini in his hand, and the Jaguar team painted the Land Rover exec as a guy who looked like a hayseed with his green wellies and Barbour jacket. "After a while," says Fields, "the whole room was laughing. It's hard to dislike or not trust somebody when you know them, right? And it's easy to dislike them when you don't know them. From then on, the group worked better together. We swept away the biases they had which were preventing good communication and good teamwork."

Back at the Bower Forum, a CEO participant made a point: "What if the problem has to do with a team member not pulling their weight because of personal problems?" Managing the mental state of each team member is a difficult challenge. Leaders have enough to keep them busy without having to stay on top of what's going on in the personal lives of their employees, and there are obvious privacy issues. Yet with the

Gen-Z and millennial workforce being more sensitive to their well-being than previous generations, leaders who ignore the psychological health of their employees do so at their own peril.

The U.S. Navy's Admiral Eric Olson, a Bower Forum instructor, discovered the importance of empathy in team building when he ran the U.S. Special Operations Command, overseeing a group of warriors not known for wearing their emotions on their sleeves. When Olson would ask the top commanders of the specialized units about the condition of their people after many years of war in Afghanistan and Iraq, he would usually hear how well the teams were doing and how proud they were of their men and women. He wasn't, however, getting the same rosy picture when he and his wife traveled around and talked to the soldiers, and especially their spouses. What he did find was a "fraying around the edges" of the special operations forces. To quantify the problem, Olson set up a task force of what he called "sensing teams" that for nine months visited and interviewed soldiers, their spouses, their children, and even their children's teachers. They found cases of separation without divorce, domestic violence without a police report, kids getting in fights or failing out of school, risky off-duty behavior, and even previously unreported suicide attempts. This was hurting the capabilities and cohesion of the teams.

The task force also uncovered some policies and behaviors by SEAL leadership that were contributing to the fraying of the force. As a result, new policies were implemented to address a wide variety of factors that were eroding trust, degrading morale, preventing optimal training, causing too much family separation, and creating organizational instability. For example, a top source of frustration was the lack of stability and predictability in scheduling. Olson said some senior enlisted members would tell him, "I'll deploy for three or four of the next five Christmases if you need me to, but tell me which ones I'll be home for and then don't screw with the schedule after that." It turned out that one of the biggest sources of stress occurred when a soldier had, say, a trip to Disneyland scheduled with their family when they returned from Afghanistan but then their deployment would be unexpectedly extended. Someone in special ops would not likely complain about that, so the top commanders started holding leaders at every level accountable for the predictability of the schedule. Once a schedule was approved it couldn't be changed without the next level of command signing off on the change.

Besides making schedules more predictable, Special Operations Command built support teams of psychologists, nutritionists, physical trainers, physical therapists, and more to both improve the quality of training and readiness and accelerate the return to operational duty after injuries. Morale has improved and the numbers of divorces, dangerous behaviors, and suicides have declined. "We simply had not been paying enough attention," says Olson.

Like Navy SEAL officers, all leaders need to be more attuned to their people and what's going on in their lives. It's a tricky tightrope to walk because of privacy issues, but leaders need to find ways to be more sensitive and listen and assess the dynamics of their teams. Says Olson, "Culture management is one of the top two or three daily chores of a top leader. There's an old adage that says culture eats strategy for breakfast, but every leader needs to develop a strategy to build and sustain the optimal culture."

*Questions that help you get your
people to speak the truth:*

///

- What might I hear if I invite the critics, the truth tellers, and those who typically don't speak up to voice their opinions?

- How do we identify and avoid gaps in all relevant dimensions— personal, team dynamics, mission planning, and competitor behavior and plans?

- Do I blame people for failures versus encouraging them to rapidly learn and bounce forward?

- How do I foster dissent more effectively and include it as a stated organizational value?

- How can I invite dissenters to become part of the decision-making process, and actively ask them to speak up so they become positive influencers later during implementation?

///

In Summary

//

The best leaders build and leverage informal networks of truth tellers who keep them grounded in reality and help them understand how their people really feel. They lead to inspire, not to direct, they foster a culture of dissent by actively seeking it, and they welcome open discussion when it comes. This kind of transparency will surely unearth some failures in the organization. The question is how to bounce forward from them.

11

PRACTICE MAKING MISTAKES

D o you allow your team room for error? When that question comes up in a Bower Forum session, everyone answers, "Of course I do." When they think about it some more, though, many admit they expect their team to succeed. "Isn't it my job to minimize failures?" asked a CEO of a tech start-up. "We don't have the luxury of missteps."

Yes and no. Teams that avoid failure miss the point, because people learn as much, if not more, from mistakes as from successes. As a leader your first inclination when things go awry may be to place blame— "Who's responsible for this?"—when you should be looking for underlying reasons for the failure. If you start out in one direction and the facts soon suggest that path is a mistake, you have to have the flexibility to change course while asking, "What can we learn? Where are we vulnerable?" The twentieth-century economist John Maynard Keynes stands as one of history's greats, in part because he had the confidence and mental agility to change his opinions. When a critic accused him of being inconsistent, Keynes reportedly retorted, "When the facts change, I change my mind. What do you do, sir?"

The eleventh element of our leadership process, "Adopt Fearless Learning," stresses the importance of flexibility, open-mindedness, and the ability to adapt to changing circumstances. When leaders and their teams take a risk and fail, which inevitably happens at some point, they need to learn from their mistakes and rapidly adjust to the new circumstances. Often leaders fall in love with a strategy or an idea and pursue it to the end, even if it becomes clear that it is not working. Typically, this is because once you've committed to a plan and invested time and effort, it's extremely difficult to change course. You might fear that you'll look weak or indecisive to your colleagues or that they'll think you weren't smart enough to come up with the right plan in the first place.

Business leaders too often stick to the patterns and plans that made them successful and fail to change when circumstances shift. By contrast, the best leaders take an unbiased look at the world around them and engage in fearless learning and encourage their teams to do the same. In other words, you should not be afraid when you learn something that contradicts your plan. When people win it's because they are not afraid to fail. They give it a shot; they show up and try something new. They're looking ahead—not back.

Putting fear aside and adapting to dynamic conditions is something retired admiral Eric Olson understands well. As a coach at the Bower Forum, he helps attendees become more agile and nimble when circumstances change in their business or in the world. Olson learned the value of flexibility while serving in the military. As the head of the U.S. Special Operations Command, he was the senior military adviser in the CIA situation room the night of the bin Laden raid, along with CIA director Leon Panetta, who had been put in charge of the operation by President Obama. Vice Admiral Bill McRaven was the Afghanistan-based operational commander. The mission was not perfect by any means, but it was successful, largely because the operators in the air and on the ground were highly adept at adjusting the plan in response to changing circumstances.

Olson later said, "The aircrews and SEAL teams must have the right equipment and finely honed skills, of course, but the key is they are composed of individuals who can unhesitatingly fall out of love with the primary plan and shift to a backup plan or develop a new one. If the map says one thing and the terrain turns out to be different, they follow the terrain, not the map."

Olson knows from experience that you can train and train to get it right, but inevitably things go wrong. What is needed is quick thinking and a mindset that allows you to rapidly overcome your hardwired tendency to stick with the original plan. In the early morning hours of May 2, 2011, two dozen Navy SEALs flying in a pair of specialized Black Hawk helicopters descended on a darkened compound in Abbottabad, Pakistan, where Osama bin Laden, the mastermind of the September 11, 2001, attacks, was in hiding. Before the team hit the ground, the plan had already gone awry when one of the helicopters crashlanded in a vacant lot next door. The other helicopter diverted to a preplanned site, also outside the main compound. Coming up with a new plan on the fly, the two SEAL teams breached the wall of bin Laden's compound at different locations, which meant careful coordination between the two teams as they ran toward each other in the total darkness, knowing that armed enemies were present. "This was real-time adjustment of the plan in its most intense form," says Olson, "and they pulled it off brilliantly." The crashed helicopter was destroyed with explosives in order to protect classified technologies, bin Laden was killed, injured civilians were medically treated, and lots of computers and documents were seized before the extraction helicopters swooped in to recover the teams. The United States suffered no fatalities that day. The mission on the ground took a mere forty minutes.

The precision and the quick, on-the-spot thinking that the Navy SEALs displayed that night during the bin Laden raid have been well documented. What isn't as well known is that the raid was the culmination of years of training for mistakes so that when it counted, each team member could take the initiative and own a mission, a problem, or a project, adjusting to things that didn't go as planned. This works because the leaders' trust in their subordinates to do the right thing is near absolute. In the corporate world, too many times well-meaning leaders can't resist jumping in and solving problems for their team. This can demotivate and disempower individuals, who then hesitate to act boldly. The best leaders know that the job of a team leader is to put the right members in place, give them the tools to do the job, and then remove any obstacles that might prevent them from solving the problem at hand. But that's not enough. As a leader, you must allow your team to make mistakes in order to learn from them. You must expect mistakes to be made and have contingency plans to recover from them. You must accept that even without mistakes, circumstances will change.

A team, of course, is only as good as its members, so selecting people with the right physical aptitude and psychological profile is crucial. Olson says that when assembling a team, it pays to look for problem solvers who are also optimists. The Navy once conducted a study to find out why the attrition rate in SEAL training was so high. About 75 percent of candidates literally rang a brass bell that hangs near the training ground when they couldn't take the grueling drills any longer. The number shouldn't have been that high, because all the people who walked in the front door were theoretically capable of graduating, having already been through a careful screening process. Some candidates failed to keep up with the physical or academic demands of the course, but the largest group of dropouts voluntarily quit not in the middle of some really hard, wet, or cold event but soon after breakfast or lunch when they were warm and dry.

The Navy discovered that these candidates dropped out because they *anticipated* that they might fail the next challenge or drill, such as a long run or swim or lying cold and wet for hours in the sand. "It was an epiphany for me," says Olson, "that people would give up a lifelong dream because they feared failure and not because they actually failed." Interestingly, the findings of the study didn't lead the Navy to change its SEAL training regimen very much, and to this day the attrition rate has stayed high. "We determined," says Olson, "that if people were quitting because they were afraid to face real conditions, it was good that we discovered that under controlled circumstances rather than when lives or mission success depended on them. If they quit during a fair and equal training and testing environment, then we weren't too sorry to see them go."

So the 25 percent who made it were optimistic risk-takers, not afraid of failure, and had a proclivity for success. Many of them were competitive water polo players or wrestlers in high school or college, but the real surprise was that many of the successful candidates were also chess players. In fact, those quality athletes who also played chess were much more likely to become a Navy SEAL than those who didn't, because they were good problem solvers. "Chess players don't quit at lunch because there's going to be a fourteen-mile run that afternoon," says Olson. "They are thinking several moves ahead, figuring out what they are going to do next week and next month and after they graduate. They are strategic thinkers and problem solvers not only in the moment but also for the next event and the one after that."

The other characteristic the Navy found among successful SEAL candidates is that no matter how tough the challenge, they would keep trying to find a solution. As Olson puts it, "We look for people who know that there's always a way to solve a problem." He could have been talking about himself. When he was a kid growing up in Tacoma, Washington, Olson, who loved to swim in the cold waters of the Pacific Northwest, wanted a wetsuit but couldn't afford it. The income from his paper route wasn't enough to buy one. But it was enough to buy two bags of neoprene scraps and eight cans of wetsuit glue from Harvey's Dive Shop in Seattle. He cut and glued dozens of scraps together to make his first wetsuit, the only one he had before he joined the Navy.

A key aspect of dealing with failure is being able to rebound under extreme pressure. In the SEALs' underwater competency test, for example, instructors intentionally create challenges for the trainees, pulling off their masks, turning off their air, or weighing them down with additional weights. A number of the candidates failed to remain underwater for the required twenty minutes. To help raise the passing rate, the Navy then created a decision-making system called "The Big Four." These are:

1. **Goal setting:** Break big challenges into easily accomplished micro-goals—first slip your mask back on and then worry about the air hose. As you finish one after another, your confidence builds.
2. **Mental rehearsal:** Visualize a fear or a challenge (like being attacked underwater or giving a big corporate presentation) over and over until it feels familiar and therefore becomes easier to handle under duress.
3. **Self-talk:** When under stress, learn to stop talking to yourself in a panicked voice and switch to a calmer, more reasonable tone, one that can help you solve problems.
4. **Stay calm:** When you feel overwhelmed by stress, try to slow your breathing and try to center yourself.

After trainees were exposed to "The Big Four," passing rates for the underwater drill rose by a third. When a high-performance team makes the right decisions in a stressful situation with many unknowns, it is no accident. They are intellectually curious—always analyzing the situation and challenging ideas. The more a team prepares itself for tough challenges, the easier it is to deviate from what was planned and solve an unexpected problem. In the SEALs they call this the MRI approach. In medicine, an MRI slices a body into hundreds of parts to see what might be wrong with one of those slices. In the SEALs, the leaders "slice" every mission plan chronologically from beginning to end in order to anticipate what might go wrong and then prepare for those eventualities.

Because the cost of making mistakes is high and public, Olson created a sense of belonging by offering a safe space for a person to take risks and fail. He created learning drills (like practicing the raid at a replica of the bin Laden compound) and instilled a focus on character and humility by stressing that team members had to be agile enough to pivot when the circumstances demanded it. That doesn't mean that there's no accountability. After a mission, Olson had his teams do a rigorous postmortem to see where the team fell short and extracted those learnings for future missions. Where an individual clearly failed on the mission, the team would discuss how to restore trust. Of course, if your team is not composed of people in the first place who have the right character attributes and values, these trust-building discussions are bound to fall short. In the corporate context this is hugely applicable and rarely done.

So, plan for success but be ready for anything. This holds for the business world as well. At Amazon, for example, the development teams write memos every time they pitch an idea. The memos can be no longer than six pages and are written in the form of a hypothetical press release, typically laying out the long-term impact of the new project and why it might appeal to a customer. An FAQ section then lays out the nuts and bolts of the project, including the market, the price, the features, and the manufacturing process. Teams at Amazon toil over these reports, constantly fine-tuning them until the day comes when they present the idea to the top brass. Amazon founder Jeff Bezos makes everyone spend the first twenty minutes of the meeting reading the report, to make sure everyone is up to speed. Then the project is vigorously challenged and debated. Flaws aren't seen as mistakes. The team's job is to expose ideas to scrutiny so that weaknesses are identified early in the process. If an Amazonian finds a flaw in the original concept or a better solution, they acknowledge it and then make the change on the fly. If the project gets the green light, the six-page memo serves as a template to keep the project on track—as the product or service progresses the team keeps referring to the memo to make sure they are staying true to the original concept. Megahits ranging from the Kindle to Fire TV to Alexa were all born with the aid of the six-pager.

"All this talk about teams learning from mistakes sounds good on paper," said one CEO who recently oversaw the merger of two companies. "But what if people simply don't agree?" He told us about how dissenting views on his team stalled an important project at his company while they argued about the direction.

When it comes to conflict among team members, Admiral Olson believes that expressing a variety of opinions and vigorous debate are essential. "I believe in the greatest possible diversity of experiences and perspectives," he says, "because sometimes the most important view is held by the least obvious person. A Navy SEAL adage is that no one is too junior to have the best idea, and no one is too senior to be wrong."

Olson adds, though, "Everyone gets a *voice* in the process, but only those who will be held accountable for the outcome get a *vote*. And once the decision is made, anyone who cannot subscribe to it needs to be removed from the team. It's up to the leader to think beyond the way things have always been done and find a solution that will propel the project or organization forward." In the case of the bin Laden raid, President Obama was presented with a wide range of options, including air-dropped bombs and missiles fired from helicopters or drones, any of which would have been the safer approach. He decided that a special ops raid would be best because it would allow verification of the identity of the Al-Qaeda leader and enable the collection of valuable intelligence materials from laptops, cell phones, and documents. As the person who would be held accountable for the outcome, he overrode many of his advisers with his decision to authorize a helicopter insertion of ground forces.

Questions to ask yourself to gauge whether you and your organization are fast learners:

///

- How do I balance my certainty about the company's strategies and major initiatives with flexibility, open-mindedness, and the ability to adapt to changing circumstances?

- How do I look at mistakes as a doorway to learning and have a process to help people improve from their mistakes?

- Do I invest sufficiently in building the same capabilities in my leaders?

- Have I created team learning rituals like postmortems to harvest the learning from our mistakes and spread them in the organization?

- Have I given people a safe space to take personal risk, inviting external perspectives and truth telling?

- Do I invite healthy opposition and search for missing perspectives to identify risks and create experiments to test and learn, knowing that fast failure is likely?

- How do I establish a culture of fearless learning, one with a permanent readiness to question and revise deep and long-held beliefs and assumptions?

///

In Summary

///

The best leaders understand the importance of flexibility, open-mindedness, and the ability to adapt to changing circumstances. They know that mistakes are doorways to learning and that making mistakes without learning is failure. They create team trust, giving people a safe space to take personal risk, inviting external perspectives and truth telling, and setting a high bar on character and humility. They invite healthy opposition and search for missing perspectives to identify risks and create experiments to test and learn, knowing that fast failure is likely. They create learning rituals like postmortems to harvest learnings and bounce forward. This requires a foundation of psychological safety that is not at the cost of accountability—balancing candor and caring.

For all this emphasis on top team performance, however, many CEOs forget the cardinal rule of leadership—people yearn to be recognized as human beings.

12

Instill Empathy

FOR PEOPLE TO CARE, SHOW THEM YOU CARE

Bob Chapman, the CEO of the manufacturing firm Barry-Wehmiller and a coach of the Bower Forum, asked attendees at a recent session a simple question: "What are you most proud of in your life, and when you leave this earth, what do you want them to say about your life?"

One participant, the CEO of a major corporation, didn't hesitate. He replied that he had given $120 million to his alma mater to establish a scholarship. Chapman replied, "That's wonderful," and asked why it was so meaningful to him. "With my scholarship students, I can be hands-on," the CEO said. "I mentor them. It's more than me giving money. It's about giving back. When one student wanted to drop out, I arranged for a tutor. I write recommendation letters for potential employers. On some days, it feels like another job, but I always go to bed knowing I made a difference."

Chapman asked him how many students the scholarship program

helps each year. "Four or five" was the answer. Chapman then asked how many people worked in his company. "Around a hundred thousand."

"The attention you give those four or five students is admirable," said Chapman. "But what about the hundred thousand people that come into your plants and offices around the world every day—how do you show them that you care?" Now it was the CEO's turn to put down his wine-glass. "Of course I care about my employees." Then, after a long pause, he added, "But I never thought of it that way."

That's when another attendee chimed in. "Everyone says they care about their people, but what does it really mean? I keep throwing money and benefits at them and they keep quitting." Chapman replied, "They're not quitting because of the pay or the benefits. You have to look in the mirror and see the way you treat your employees."

Chapman has made it his mission to encourage leaders to embrace our twelfth leadership element, "Instill Empathy." He knows that although most executives will say that people come first, putting people first in the real world is hard to do and requires skills and courage to genuinely care.

It is, however, worth the extra effort. McKinsey's 2023 report "Performance Through People" analyzed eighteen hundred large companies across all sectors in fifteen countries and found that a sharp focus on financials coupled with an emphasis on developing human capital leads to sustained outperformance. Putting people first does not come at the expense of financial results. In fact, it boosts them. Those companies that develop systems and habits aimed at putting people first stand to boost their bottom lines over the long term—while delivering benefits for their employees as well. As the McKinsey report put it, "At a time of uncertainty and talent scarcity, leaders can choose to capture lasting benefits by ensuring that their organizations truly work for their people."

Caring for people pays off in another way. The high-performing companies in the McKinsey study that emphasized both financials and people development enjoyed an attrition rate 5 percentage points lower than those companies that focused mainly on financials. Not only do employees leave the results-only-oriented companies at a higher rate, but these firms fire more frequently, which suggests either that they aren't good at hiring people who are a good fit or they aren't getting the most out of those they bring on board.

High-performing companies such as the retailer Costco, Google, and the outdoor clothing company Patagonia have thrived in part by treating their employees well. Costco's generous wages and benefits and supportive work environment have resulted in low turnover rates and high employee satisfaction numbers. Famously, Google has provided free meals, on-site gyms, and other perks to help its employees stay happy and healthy. Patagonia offers flexible work schedules, on-site childcare, and a generous time-off policy. According to the research firm Great Places to Work, *91 percent* of employees at Patagonia say it is a great place to work, compared with 57 percent of employees at a typical U.S.-based company.

While providing perks, pay, and benefits is necessary, it is not sufficient when it comes to building a truly compassionate workplace. Leaders must listen to the worries, needs, and frustrations of their workers and then find ways to assuage those concerns. Whenever possible they should get to know their employees and do everything within reason to make sure they are faring well. This might mean giving them extra slack when someone or their family gets hit with a health problem, or finding ways to smooth over conflicts in the workplace, including dealing with supervisors whose behavior is impacting the productivity and mental well-being of others. It means making sure people are taken care of as if they're your own family.

This is hard, time-consuming work for anyone—never mind a stretched-to-the-max CEO. Research shows, however, that such efforts fall to the bottom line. McKinsey's most recent Organizational Health Index survey looked at employee burnout and a company's overall health. The survey found that while companies with bottom-quartile health had a 68 percent burnout rate, the top quartile only had a 25 percent burnout rate. That's still high, but low enough to give them a performance edge. In fact, the top-quartile companies over a five-year period enjoyed nearly a three times higher total return to shareholders than those in the middle quartiles. Burnout is an indication that people are not cared for and are not getting what they need. When an organization suffers from a high percentage of burnout, inevitably it is not benefiting from people performing at their best.

Moreover, McKinsey's "Performance Through People" report found that companies that outperformed others by putting emphasis on both finances and people know that bosses and supervisors play an outsize role in determining employees' job satisfaction, which in turn affects their well-being. Sadly, three-quarters of respondents in one recent survey said that the most stressful aspect of their job was their immediate boss. Frontline and mid-level managers are particularly important, and people often need training to step into these roles. One way to ensure effective leadership and stop a leader's bad tendencies from harming morale or effectiveness is creating a system of 360-degree feedback. Another way is for the CEO and the executive team to set an example by finding ways to show that they truly care about their people. The most effective leaders listen as much as they talk, recognizing that good ideas (and the next generation of leadership) often come from those on the front lines. They consciously follow an approach that enables employees to speak up, not only to involve them in establishing the companies' vision and offer ideas, but also to state frankly when things are not working.

In Bob Chapman's case, he has the hard numbers to prove that creating human and economic value in harmony—not in sacrifice of each other—is in fact the right way to lead an organization. Since he took over Barry-Wehmiller (BW) from his father in 1975, Chapman transformed this struggling $18 million in revenue maker of machinery for the beer industry by diversifying into other markets through the acquisition of more than 140 businesses and never selling one. Today, the St. Louis company takes in $3.5 billion a year in revenue and employs some thirteen thousand team members around the globe. Although the company is private, Chapman says its equity share price has risen more than 10 percent a year for more than two decades.

Chapman came upon his people-centric philosophy the hard way—he committed some bad business mistakes. When his father died in 1975, Chapman inherited a St. Louis business that made bottle washers and pasteurizers for Anheuser-Busch and other beer makers. In the early 1980s the beer companies, suffering from excess capacity, cut back on orders and started buying their machinery on pure price rather than relationships. From 1983 through 1987, Chapman, who had earned an MBA from the University of Michigan, lived on the edge of bankruptcy. His banks pulled their credit lines, and he had to take out a loan from an asset-based lender, which he says is like "borrowing money from a guy in a dark alley with an envelope." Although he was proud of the history of the company, he realized its history did not give it a viable future.

To grow, he had to diversify out of the beverage industry. Although he had no experience or financial resources, he began acquiring a diversified portfolio of businesses in packaging machinery—product lines that no one else wanted and where the sellers would virtually finance the sale. "I developed a new business model," says Chapman, "that had more focus on recurring revenue with little customer, technology, or market concentration so that any one market could change, and we would be okay." The gambit worked. His company was doing well.

But Chapman knew he could do better. Once he had built what he calls his Ferrari-engine business model, he needed premium gasoline to run it. He turned to his people. In 2000, he had his first big revelation. He had acquired a South Carolina manufacturer and flown there to be on hand for the first day of the new ownership. It was during March Madness, and everybody was betting on their college basketball teams getting into the Final Four. Chapman watched as some of the employees, who were on a coffee break, talked about the outcome of basketball games and how they were doing in the pool. "I was just having a cup of coffee," recalls Chapman, "and thinking about how I just bought this company, and I was going to sit down with the customer service team and have a talk. I had no agenda. Then I noticed that the closer we got to our 8:00 a.m. start time, the more you could see the fun go out of the bodies as people had to go to work." When Chapman sat down with the dozen people in the customer service group, out of nowhere he said, "We're going to play our own March Madness game. Whoever sells the most spare parts each week will win $100, and whichever team sells the most will get $100."

The employees told Chapman there were twenty reasons they couldn't do that, but because he was the new owner and he wanted them to have fun, the game was on. That week revenue went up by 20 percent, but according to Chapman, joy went up by 1,000 percent. Instead of just coming in every day and entering sales orders, they came in every day to win as a team and as individuals. One woman on the team told Chapman, "I always thought I was nice to the customers but now I'm really nice."

Fascinated by the result, Chapman tried the experiment in a few other areas of the company and soon saw the positive impact of aligning value creation with having fun. "I said, 'Something is going on here bigger than this.'" He gathered his top twenty executives to create a set of leadership principles inspired by what they were experiencing. The exec team came up with a one-page checklist that included a dozen principles designed to create more dignity in the workplace, such as:

- I inspire passion, optimism, and purpose.
- My personal communication cultivates fulfilling relationships.
- I proactively engage in the personal growth of individuals on my team.

"We looked at it like the Declaration of Independence and the U.S. Constitution rolled into one," says Chapman. "One of our leaders said, 'A lot of companies have inspirational visions on the wall, but they don't live them.'" The CEO replied, "We are not going to put them on the wall. We are going to put them in people's hearts and minds." Chapman began doing just that by flying around the country and sharing their guiding principles of leadership and asking people if they were living those values.

During a visit to one of his factories in northern Wisconsin, which employed five hundred people, the leaders complained to Chapman that when he talked about his guiding principles, everyone would get inspired, but by the next day they would gravitate back to their traditional practices. They wanted to know how they could keep the spirit alive when he wasn't there preaching. At the time, Chapman, who is a car enthusiast, owned a bright yellow Chevy SSR retro pickup truck. He told the factory leaders to have the workers vote for the employee whose behavior aligned most with the organization's values—how they treated other people and their customers—and that person would get to drive the SSR for a week.

Letting an employee drive a fancy car for a week might sound patronizing, but it had a huge impact on morale at the factory. While the shiny yellow truck was sitting outside the plant, the team leaders announced the winner of the vote: Mary, who worked in the accounting department. She stood onstage as her colleagues read statements praising her. She took the keys to the car and started crying as her husband walked out from behind the stage with her two kids, the rector of her church, and her brother-in-law, who were all there to see Mary be recognized for her goodness. Chapman realized not only that this kind of recognition was profoundly meaningful to the winner, but also that it was having a dramatic impact on everyone present as they witnessed the family react to their loved one being honored.

Chapman has repeated these recognition ceremonies some five hundred times—using different types of fun cars—around his empire. One winner told him, "Mr. Chapman, it was the most profound recognition of my life and the first thing I did was call my spouse to tell him I won. The second thing is I drove the car over to take my mother for a ride."

Another winner, who worked in the IT department, told him, "I took my daughter for a ride in the Virginia foothills with that car, and at least thirty people stopped me when I was at the gas station, at the tollbooth, and at the drive-in restaurant and asked, 'Why do you have that car?' and I said, 'Well, I won it for my good attitude at work.' They would say, 'I wish I worked for a company like that.'" She also added, "Mr. Chapman, unfortunately my mother is dead, but I want you to know I did drive the car by the cemetery to show my mother I won."

This kind of recognition and celebration has become part of the DNA of the Barry-Wehmiller company. Yet the reverberations go beyond morale. Stress is one of the leading causes of absenteeism and turnover. Some 74 percent of all illnesses or chronic diseases can be linked to stress. People who love their job have 40 percent fewer health care claims than people who feel the stress of meeting the numbers or of being downsized. It's no coincidence that heart attacks are 20 percent more frequent on Monday mornings than at other times. BW saw its people get healthier as workplace dignity improved—its health care costs are less than the industry average. In an economy where it's hard to hire skilled workers, the company had no problem attracting talent.

Then the 2008 financial crisis hit. Chapman told his board that the company had a strong backlog of orders and didn't need to lay anyone off. The board told him he was being too optimistic, and they proved to be right. While on a business trip to Italy in 2009, Chapman received an email that one of his biggest customers had put a major order on hold. Shocked, he sat down in his hotel room and began weighing the implications. "I thought about how we measure success by the way we touch the lives of people, and if we let people go, we're going to hurt people badly because there were no jobs out there. For people who've gotten laid off or downsized, it is one of the lowest points in their life because they have to go home to their families and say, 'I don't know how we're going to get through because I just got let go.'"

He then had a eureka moment. Chapman figured that if everyone in the company gave up a month's pay, he wouldn't have to lay anyone off. Obviously, many workers couldn't afford to lose that income, so Chapman set up a barter system where older, better-off employees could trade some unpaid time off with someone struggling financially and who couldn't afford to lose any pay. People could trade as much unpaid time off as they wanted with others, as long as in the end the total payroll savings that year added up to that one-twelfth cut.

Back in the States, Chapman announced the program and got an overwhelming response.

BW's employees knew that they were going to lose one-twelfth of their pay, but they traded that for job security. "A person," says Chapman, "could look at Mary and Bill on either side of them and say, 'By taking some unpaid time off, I just helped Mary or Bill keep their job and I know how much they needed the money.'" The company made it through the Great Recession without any layoffs and came out of the economic crisis stronger, validating its culture of caring and retaining its talent. If Chapman had not been preaching his guiding principles of leadership for several years, he would not have thought of this alternative to layoffs as a way of dealing with financial crisis.

In this tough situation, Chapman succeeded because he was able to balance caring and candor. He told his people what he was going to do about layoffs, and he figured out the most humane solution given the circumstances. An organization with a lot of caring but not enough candor will not perform well because there's no direct feedback, no truth telling, and a lack of accountability. On the other hand, too much candor without enough caring is no better because it builds a culture riddled with anxiety and fear, and one that hides mistakes. The best leaders know that caring does not have to be at the cost of candor.

The key here is thinking about an employee as someone's precious child and treating them as you would like your child treated. Managers use terms like "downsizing" and "right-sizing" to dehumanize the process. It makes them feel better when they attend a cocktail party and their Sunday morning service. Yet the process is inhumane—in a mass firing, security shows up and makes sure people don't steal anything while they empty out their desks. "If we measure success by the way we touch people's lives," says Chapman, "and then we lay off hundreds of people, destroying their lives, how can we say we care about each other?" There is collateral damage too. "You might keep your job during a downsizing, but if the person sitting next to you loses hers and she's a single mother on a tight budget, you say to yourself that you could be next. So you live with this higher level of anxiety and stress because there's no sense of security or safety for your income." So what matters is less *what* you do but *how* you do it. Showing genuine care, creating space to listen and process strong emotions in tough times is what matters most.

There are instances where Chapman had to transition someone out of the organization, but only after giving that person many chances to improve. "I don't like the term to 'fire' someone," he says, "because it comes from the French, who invented the firing squad—you line up people to shoot them. What we do is called strict parenting or tough love." When someone isn't performing, the leaders at BW have the patience to coach that person until they change, which is what happens in most situations. Chapman likens it to a bus traveling in a circuit. Every once in a while the bus pulls up and the driver asks if you would like to join the journey. The person might say they're not ready a few times, but eventually they'll step on board. It's not a workers' utopia, however. "We sometimes have to address the situation," says Chapman, "where a person is actually upsetting other people, but we address it in a human way as if we were trying to help our own troubled son or daughter." He calls this practice "courageous patience."

The transition from management to leadership became an intentional journey for the leaders of BW. Within the company, Chapman created BW University, which trains leaders about the company's values, including how to listen to and respect people. He created the university because one of his greatest fears is that his focus on caring would die with him, as often happens to successful companies or movements when an inspirational leader retires or passes away. To create disciples, Chapman has all his leaders at BW take intensive courses. As he explains, "Every day that I get on our corporate jet, the pilots have rigorously gone through a checklist to make sure that when I put my foot in that aircraft, they have done everything they could possibly do to protect my safety. I thought, 'Why don't we create a leadership checklist so that every time somebody sets their foot in one of our buildings around the world, the leaders make sure that every soul is safe?' So we created what we called the leadership checklist—things you need to think about every day as a leader to be a good steward of the lives entrusted to you."

Some of the most important items on the checklist are listening, recognition, and celebration—all hallmarks of a leader who is empathetic, humble, and learns how to listen to their people's concerns and then let them know in timely, thoughtful ways that they matter. BW University also teaches what's called a "culture of service" to encourage leaders to find opportunities to serve others. It's a similar idea to what's used in the U.S. military, which honors those who give themselves in service of others—as opposed to in the business world, which rewards people who sacrifice others in service of themselves.

BW University has been paying dividends outside the business as well. One woman who ran BW's personnel department in Minneapolis told Chapman that she had just taken the three-day listening class and it changed her life. "It opened my mind and heart," she told Chapman. "Now I know how to better raise my two-year-old daughter. Now my teenage daughters are talking to me, and I have a stronger relationship with my dad." "Stories like this," says Chapman, "have shown us that the way we lead impacts the way people live. That is why leadership is such an awesome responsibility."

BW team members learn human skills like listening, how to recognize and celebrate others, and how to embrace a culture of service—subjects rarely taught in our universities. "We live in a society where success is viewed as money, power, and position. And yet with a vibrant global economy, we have an epidemic of anguish and a poverty of dignity because we don't know how to care for others in our community, homes, and workplaces. The greatest act of charity is not the checks we write to noble causes; the greatest act of charity is how we treat those under our care."

Chapman believes that for Truly Human Leadership—BW's name for the leadership philosophy Chapman has championed—to become mainstream, it must start with schools and universities embracing a new vision for creating tomorrow's leaders. He is working with several university business schools as well as a private primary school, showing them how to embrace the human skills that are the foundation of Truly Human Leadership. "We are self-destructing as a society for economic gain because we think money is the source of happiness and we know it is not," says Chapman. "We need to start creating leaders who have the skills and the courage to care for the people they will have the privilege of leading."

Chapman recalls his own traditional business school education and early experience, which taught him to view people in his organization as merely functions for his own success. His journey from traditional business leader to a more human-centered leader came as a result of a revelation that caused him to see those in his care not as functions, but as someone's precious child. "It is my responsibility," says Chapman, "to make sure everyone feels safe and valued in their roles, and that I provide them with a grounded sense of hope for the future."

Few CEOs would disagree with Chapman. The question is, will they rise to the occasion? Showing people you care usually costs very little, yet leaders struggle because it requires them to get out of their bubble. Also, it is an investment in which it's hard to prove the ROI. To many it feels like a second priority, or worse, a waste of time and money. That's the wrong approach. You're not going to succeed unless your people care about the long-term success of the company, and for them to feel that way they need to see you treat each of them as a person, not just an "employee" to execute your to-do list. They need to see your spark, your interest, your attention. Once you show your team how much you value them and that you care about their long-term success, there's nothing they won't strive to accomplish.

It's an age-old truth that most people like to be recognized and appreciated for their effort. In business this is especially important for employee morale, as we've seen in the case of Bob Chapman, and the recognition programs he established at Barry-Wehmiller. A Gallup poll released in 2023 found that in companies with strong recognition programs, employees were less likely to leave, were 73 percent less likely to "always" or "very often" feel burned out, and four times as likely to be actively engaged in their work.

Yet in organizations—especially ones with large numbers of employees—giving your people individual attention is not an easy act to pull off. How can leaders recognize so many people in an authentic way when the weight of the top job is bringing constant demands for their time and attention? In addition to that, every individual has different personal needs. So leaders need to learn to treat different people differently. As much as possible, they have to learn to read them psychologically. They need to know that Sally might respond well to tough love, but George has to be handled with kid gloves because if you say a harsh word he's going to be upset and clam up.

As Rob Painter, the CEO of Trimble, puts it, "We've got about thirteen thousand people who work here and there are thirteen thousand different life stories and thirteen thousand different personalities. This individuality has been something that's been, let's say, underappreciated." During the pandemic, Painter started checking in more with his employees over Zoom calls. He says that the pandemic opened his eyes to the different challenges and experiences some of his employees were going through. "I saw," he says, "that their life experience could be wildly different than mine." He started to better appreciate individual differences and began to think about how to integrate that quality into his leadership style.

As he began to think about it, he realized that his thirteen direct reports all have different needs and desires for personal connection. From some 360-degree evaluations, Painter learned that some of his executives longed for more personal connection from him. This was somewhat of a surprise for him because his own need for personal connection was easily met. When talking with someone, he liked to dive straight into work. For others, he learned that wasn't the case. They wanted to take the time to talk about their weekend or their kids before getting to the task at hand. "I wasn't seeing it," says Painter, "because there's this human tendency where we all have a filter of how we experience life and we tend to think that everybody has the same filter we do, but they don't. I now spend more time trying to see people as individuals."

To find out what makes them tick, Painter literally asks them what they need in terms of personal connection. Some of his team members felt very comfortable with very little personal connection, and then there were two who wanted more, and Painter obliged. "I think if you're authentic," he says, "you can pull this off. But if you ask, 'How was your weekend?' and you don't really care, that will do more harm than good." Leaders, of course, are busy, and often don't have time to engage in personal conversations. In those instances, Painter says to those who desire more personal connection, "I've only got a few minutes," or "I've got a quick question for you." That way the person knows you're strapped for time and is less likely to feel neglected.

Learning to be more aware of the individuals who work for you isn't easy. It takes excess mental capacity to understand everybody's story beyond the friendly exchange of "How's it going?" at the start of meetings. To listen to personal stories in an authentic way and then refer to some of those stories when you meet an individual again requires great mental capacity. If you, say, listen to the life story of a new hire and then bump into them a year later, they will expect you to remember who they are. If you don't, they will certainly be disappointed, if not demoralized. Sometimes you just have to be authentic and say, "What's your name again and what are you working on?" Painter says in those situations he tries to make light of it by saying, "I'm having a senior moment."

Your odds of remembering employees' names and their kids' names and what they're working on increases, says Painter, if you work at being present in the moment. "I'm at my best when I'm mindful and engaged, which is to say I'm not multitasking or multitasking in my head. I go to business reviews with no computer or phone, just a notebook and a pen. The challenge is to limit the distractions as much as possible. I got rid of social media, and I even took LinkedIn off my phone. The fallacy of multitasking is, it ends up taking longer than if you would have just focused on one thing, because when you are present, you're in an active intellectual and emotional processing mode."

As we've seen, CEOs have so much power that the words they use and the level of care they show can impact employee morale dramatically. The challenge is to use that power mindfully.

FOR PEOPLE TO CARE, SHOW THEM YOU CARE

———

While it's important to recognize individuals in your day-to-day work, what do you do when your company has three hundred thousand employees? You can't possibly connect with them all, especially those toiling on the front lines and interacting with customers every day. To raise morale at this kind of scale, Frank D'Souza, the former CEO of the IT services firm Cognizant, focused on what he calls "heroes, rituals, and legends." In his early days as CEO, D'Souza realized that his company was growing so fast that 60 percent of Cognizant's employees had been at the company for only eighteen months or less. "I said to myself," he recalls, "that if this trend continues, we're going to completely lose our culture." The young CEO started doing some reading and deep thinking on culture and eventually came across an obscure academic paper that concluded that culture gets promulgated by the heroes, rituals, and legends of an organization.

"Heroes, rituals, and legends" became his go-to model for promulgating culture, because it seemed authentic. "You can write a value statement and hang it on the wall, but it doesn't really work," says D'Souza. "You need a lot more." So he and his executive team put in a concerted effort to identify the heroes and legends among their three hundred thousand employees, and to create rituals where they could set the example for others. "The idea," he says, "was to embed our values in the rituals." In one small example of a ritual, D'Souza tried to quickly answer every email he was sent, regardless of whether it came from his largest client or his newest frontline employee. It was a habit he learned from his mother, who valued the importance of connections and the preservation of relationships when the family moved from place to place. These quick responses sent the signal that every person at Cognizant

205

was important. The practice caught on and leaders across the company began to show their people the same attention and service-oriented approach that was already the norm for how they served customers.

On a larger scale, he set up rituals where the company celebrated its people who behaved in ways that fit the company's values. In the IT service industry, the most important factor is the quality of the projects you do for your clients—in Cognizant's case it included upgrading enterprise computing systems, helping clients convert to cloud computing, and many other critical technological tasks. D'Souza wanted to find a way to drive customer and employee satisfaction simultaneously. Instead of writing value statements and memos stressing the importance of project quality, D'Souza created a ritual that generated heroes. Called "Project of the Year," the ritual was a highly competitive process where teams submitted the project that they thought was best of class across a series of dimensions, including high customer satisfaction, technical excellence, and on-time delivery. Outside judges would pick the project of the year as well as the employee of the year from across the entire company, and then Cognizant would celebrate these heroes by, in one instance, renting a cricket stadium where sixty thousand of Cognizant's employees and family members would cheer the winners.

"This ritual made the winners feel good," says D'Souza, "but that wasn't the point. The real benefit was that sixty thousand employees and their families looked down on that stage and said, 'How do I get there next year, and what do I have to do to emulate that behavior to get there next year?' There was no money, just a piece of paper, but it became a very powerful way to get people engaged." In other words, to get people to care, show that you care.

Leaders need to be able to balance doing the hard things in a human way. They need to take courageous action and be candid in feedback, and to do this compassionately. The more senior you are, the tougher it is for people to see your compassion. CEOs and senior leaders often need to make difficult decisions or engage in difficult conversations. Remember that unless you show them, people who are more distant from the top will only see the difficult outcomes and not see that you care. One does not have to be at the cost of the other. The more senior you are, the more you need to consciously think about how you will demonstrate that you care.

Questions to ask yourself about instilling empathy:

- How do I balance doing the right things—even when hard—with doing them in a humane way?

- What rituals have I established to recognize people who best represent our values?

- Do I have the presence of mind and patience to listen to the personal stories of my employees in an authentic way? How do I build such empathy-based skills?

- Do I consistently infuse transparency and fairness in making personnel decisions?

- What would be included on my team's checklist when defining the elements of an empathetic leader?

- How do we as leaders sufficiently model empathy-based behaviors?

- Do I proactively engage in the personal growth of individuals on my team by expressing empathy and offering coaching?

In Summary

///

The first section of this book focused on leaders who learned how to become more compassionate and authentic human beings. The stories that you just read in part 2 were all about using those qualities to unleash the potential of people in an institution. That journey starts with an inspiring mission and a bold vision that gives people clarity and a sense of purpose. Leaders must then step back and let their people execute their tasks, while helping them build a sense of ownership and autonomy. And they must help them build the capabilities—both hard and soft—to do that. This kind of freedom works at scale only if it is backed by a system of truth telling where people don't hold things back from one another. In turn, this transparency allows the organization to naturally conduct experiments and learn from them, becoming in the process a constantly refining, collaborative, and high-performing culture. And of course, leaders have to back all of their initiatives with care and empathy—creating a safe environment where teams can feel a sense of belonging and do their best work.

Mastering the inside-out leadership approach is rewarding, but it can also be stressful and exhausting. In the next chapter, we help leaders form a "commitment plan," designed to make their continual learning and reinvention journey more disciplined and more enjoyable.

Conclusion

THE JOURNEY NEVER ENDS

The stories and insights we have shared in this book illustrate the many ways in which leaders have stepped up to reinvent themselves. Some learned to listen; others learned to learn—especially learning fearlessly and with true curiosity, always ready to question long-held beliefs and assumptions. Some put their egos aside to focus on building well-functioning teams and value for the organization. Others mustered the courage to make bold moves or change their minds when the evidence argued to the contrary. Others still took extraordinary efforts to connect with the people in their organization, more frequently and more authentically.

So where do you go from here? We've learned from running the Bower Forum programs and from working with hundreds of McKinsey clients on building leadership and reinventing companies that it would be difficult for even the very best leaders to master all at once the twelve modes of reinvention that we highlighted in this book. In fact, the modes

210

of leadership reinvention you choose will depend on your starting point as well as on internal and external factors. Every leader is different. Not only do they operate in different industries—and some in nonprofits—but they also face different situations. Overseeing an industrial turnaround requires different leadership skills than running a high-tech growth company. Every leader must analyze their particular situation and work on mastering the skills that best fit their situation and leadership style.

That said, we have found that in the life cycle of a CEO some skills are likely to be more relevant in the early years than in the middle or later years. In the early stages, the focus is on listening to all stakeholders (including customers, business partners, and board colleagues), on learning which priorities and objectives to set and figuring out how to pursue them. You will need to do all this while navigating the competing interests of stakeholders and making bold moves that will reinvent the company so it will be successful in the long term. In the middle years, complacency often sets in, and it's important to work on attributes like having a sense of purpose and being an inspiration for your fellow executives and teams (as well as for the broader organization) that help keep the energy level consistently high. In the final stage of a CEO's tenure, the emphasis will change to leaving a strong legacy, which means putting aside your ego and finding a successor who can lead the organization into the future. In any stage of a CEO's tenure, you should not underestimate the importance of selfless leadership, which entails a continued and sincere commitment to enhance your human leadership attributes.

The best CEOs know, however, that one element runs consistently through all stages of a CEO's tenure—constant reinvention and learning. They know that they're running their first lap as fast as their middle and last laps. They are constantly challenging themselves and challenging the organization. Yes, they may have made their bold move early, but they are cognizant of adding a second or third one later in their tenure, because not all market opportunities show up in your first two years.

While it's important to be aware of these stages of a leader's tenure, it's equally crucial to understand that no matter where you are on your journey, you have to try to avoid getting caught up in the frenzy of being a CEO and instead focus on constantly reflecting and reinventing yourself. This means nurturing curiosity and adopting many of the mindsets that we have discussed in the pages of this book. It requires the ability to constantly shift your balance and embrace the polarities of leadership. It means being both vulnerable and decisive, humble yet courageous, providing more space to others while not stepping away, and being both willing to change but also steadfast in the organization's values and purpose. At the same time, you have to be a system thinker able to embrace multiple perspectives and opposing ideas and understand their interdependencies, while being aware of all stakeholder concerns.

And when you're ready to leave your big job, don't think of it as the end of your journey. While it's hard for many to walk away from being a leader of a big organization and give up the perks, the attention, and the compensation (both actual and spiritual), the skills you built up over your tenure should serve you well. Chances are you will continue to do something remarkable with your life. And if you have developed the skills we explored inside this book—listening to others, unleashing the potential of your colleagues, reconciling different views and ideas, being humble, feeling you belong, and making bold moves—you will find your next meaningful opportunities sooner than you might think. Be proud of your legacy and move on.

The twelve leadership elements that we explored in depth in this book are not easy to master and take time. No one can achieve personal and professional transformation in a two-day leadership program. It is a journey that takes years, one where you have to be mindful every day about who you want to be, about the personal learning and reinvention steps you are pursuing, and what kinds of teams and organization you want to build. The good news is that it's never too early or too late to start this journey.

The vast majority of leaders whom we see through our work and the CEOs who attend the Bower Forum strive over the subsequent weeks and months to change themselves and their organizations before ultimately reinventing themselves. One Japanese CEO, for instance, walked away from the Bower Forum with a renewed sense of confidence to tackle a major organizational transformation. "The other CEOs I met there," he says, "were facing similar challenges, and that told me that I was not alone and gave me the courage to move ahead with my plan." This CEO took what he learned at our program and returned to the office knowing that he needed to master a balancing act—how to be both bold and humble and someone who sets a clear direction yet is willing to give his people the latitude to innovate and take risks.

We've also seen, however, what happens when there is no follow-through or commitment to personal, constant learning and improvements. A handful of leaders forget what they discovered about themselves and revert to their old habits—not listening, thinking they have all the answers, micromanaging their staff, and not caring enough about their people. Typically, those leaders don't last long in the top job and lose followership in their organizations over time.

That's why we suggest to our attendees that they make a commitment plan for success, to remind them of the insights they gained at these sessions. It's easy to get very motivated by what you learn at an event like ours and then lose that sense of energy and renewal when the strains of daily work pull you in multiple directions. The commitment plan needs to address the promises they made to themselves, their executive team members, and the broader organization. (This is consistent with our three-dimensional leadership approach: Lead yourself, lead your executive team, and lead your organization.) We believe that a commitment plan would also prove useful for anyone who has read this book and wants to apply what they have learned to their career.

There is no right or wrong commitment plan. Each one will be tailored to a person's own journey. The idea is to create practices that help you keep learning at the edge of your comfort zone. Because the senior leadership role in general, and the CEO role specifically, will demand so much from you, the stakes will feel high, and the responsibilities will weigh heavily. You might feel lonely at times. So go easy on yourself and indulge in a good dose of self-acceptance and self-compassion. The commitment plan is there to help you reduce stress and stay in practice, providing you with a leadership compass.

In their commitment plans, some will prioritize the steps to becoming a more human leader that we explored in part 1 of this book. Others will put at the top of their list the kind of organizational change we highlighted in part 2 of the book. Whatever the case, a commitment plan should be aspirational, itemizing the behaviors and changes that you desire both for yourself and for your organization, such as:

- I need to listen more deeply to my stakeholders and reflect on the implications of what I hear.

- I must develop a clear mandate, while taking into consideration multiple perspectives, areas of focus, and different time frames.
- I need to be more caring toward my colleagues and become a more human-centric leader.
- I have to change the culture so people in my organization will tell me what's really going on.
- I have to give my people more latitude to take the initiative.
- I need to find ways to constantly reinvent myself and be aware of the balancing act that requires those subtle changes in mindset at any given moment.

A solid commitment plan, however, goes beyond the aspirational and lists *how* you might achieve your aspirations. One crucial element of every commitment plan is to fashion a set of tools to help you advance on your journey, tools that we call micro-practices, typically structured along the lines of "lead yourself," "lead your teams," and "lead your broader organization." For example:

- **Lead yourself:** Analyze your calendar and redefine your time allocation to include these categories: professional/business, family and friends time, spiritual time (including meditation and mindfulness), and other personal time (including sleep, workout, and hobbies).
- **Lead your teams:** At the start of any interaction with someone, first check in and ask how they're doing, and really mean it (dedicate 20 percent of the scheduled meeting time for this).
- **Lead your organization:** Create a work environment that fosters creativity and experimentation. Celebrate innovative ideas

in company-wide emails, and hold innovation competitions to develop new ideas around priority topics.

We have listed one hundred of our favorite micro-practices on pages 229–45 of the appendix, which will help you cement the behaviors we've discussed, whether it's being a better listener, being more empathetic, having more energy and more courage to make bold moves, or being a more inclusive team player.

We believe it is critical to review and refresh commitment plans as external and internal factors change and as a CEO makes progress on their journey. A plan can also be helpful when it all feels like too much and when you feel overwhelmed by competing demands. That is a signal to step back and take a moment to reflect on your commitment plan.

The CEO of a large North American packaging company who attended a Bower Forum is a good example of a commitment plan in action. He knew that his company, which is private and family owned, needed a cultural transformation. The business faced a lot of challenges, from foreign competition to increasing environmental restrictions that threatened the viability of its plastic products. He needed to get the organization to move faster, take more risks, and build the skills needed to handle any number of future scenarios—some of them unknowable. But at the same time he needed to figure out how to balance respect for a strong, long-lived culture with the need for change. He was excited to get back to work with a renewed sense of energy, but one of the other CEOs at the program asked him how he planned to keep the momentum for change going once he got back to the office and became distracted by the myriad responsibilities every CEO faces.

The Bower Forum coaches and other CEOs at the program helped him draft a commitment plan on a whiteboard. This CEO returned from the Bower Forum with a plan that prioritized a clear mandate to drive long-term, profitable growth, the need for organizational change—getting his people out of their comfort zone—a big, bold move that would change the environmental footprint of his company's packaging products, and a plan to create a business operating system that strove for excellence and was designed to advance a purposeful cultural transformation. (See an example of a typical commitment plan on pages 218–19.)

The beauty of a commitment plan, this CEO says, "is that it distilled your job down to a simple picture of what your role is really all about. It's like a light bulb going on. Yes, there's obviously a lot of complexity and detail to actually make it all happen, but the commitment plan keeps you focused less on what you need to do today but on what you need to do as a leader to succeed in the long term. It helps you prepare for a range of futures that might come."

The key to designing a good commitment plan is to make sure it contains these three basic elements:

1. **Leading yourself:** Define how you want to grow your human leadership qualities. This includes learning how to balance polarities such as humility and assertiveness; being certain about what you know and being open to learning new things; and wanting to be in control with empowering teams to take the initiative. Here you should also include a section on your mandate and overall priorities.

2. **Leading your executive teams:** Write down what kinds of human leadership attributes you want to see in your executive team members and how you plan to coach them so that they can more effectively embrace the balancing acts as described in the introduction. What things can you do as CEO to act as a better role model?

3. **Leading the broader organization:** List ways you can spread your new leadership style, mindsets, behaviors, and changes in governance throughout the organization. For example, once your executive team starts embracing your leadership changes, ask *them* to act as role models to their direct reports and so forth down the line.

EXAMPLE OF A TYPICAL COMMITMENT PLAN TO CREATE LONG-TERM VALUE AND ORGANIZATIONAL HEALTH

Overarching strategic mandate: To achieve sustainable value for all stakeholders through a transformation entailing an enhanced business operating system (including digital-first operations), customer intimacy and -centricity, and a renewed product and services portfolio.

Leading yourself

1. Practice inspirational leadership (via engagement, reinforcing the vision, accessibility to people, encouraging people to unleash their potential).
2. Regularly learn from innovative leaders within and outside my industry.
3. Adopt new versatility and skills related to "profitable growth."

Leading your executive team

1. Engage my team in frank and constructive dialogue with more edge.
2. Spend 30 percent of my time dedicated to coaching.

3. Establish a succession plan with transition benchmarks over the next year.

Leading the broader organization
1. Create a more innovative culture through celebration of thoughtful risk taking.
2. Balance assertive and inclusive leadership.
3. Maintain a relentless organizational focus on customer evolving needs.

Next steps to get tactical on the strategy
1. Outline future scenarios for strategic opportunities.
2. Define what winning looks like in each scenario from multiple angles: customer, shareholders and other stakeholders, plus financials and organizational health.
3. Identify and prioritize bold moves.

Set up an operating model to drive functional excellence
1. Prioritize areas to focus on and set supporting goals.
2. Create initiatives tied to my targets.
3. Establish a mechanism for accountability.

Purposeful culture change and capability building
1. Get my people out of their comfort zone.
2. Stress rapid learning from failure.
3. Demand openness and transparency.

Once they have put their commitment plan to paper, the best leaders use their trusted circle of advisers—which typically consists of colleagues, other CEOs, friends, and outside mentors and coaches (including Bower Forum coaches)—to make sure they are holding themselves to it over the months and years. The value of outside help cannot be overstated. In our survey, nearly half of Bower Forum participants said that after they left the program, they enlisted an executive coach as a source of insight for personal reinvention. (For more survey results see pages 246–47 of the appendix.)

Whether it's with one trusted mentor or a circle of advisers, the idea is to set up a regularly scheduled meeting either monthly or quarterly where you can discuss your progress against your commitment plan. Personal change is hard, so the people you turn to need to be trusted and ones whom you admire for their leadership style, their career success, and their personal qualities—people who can be sympathetic but tough enough to help you take an unvarnished look at your progress on your journey. Ideally, such trusted advisers have successfully completed several of their own reinventions and can share relevant experiences and make suggestions for change. The idea is to create a safe space with a set of people with whom you can be open about your innermost hopes, doubts, and bold ideas. Think of it as a sounding board, where you can reflect on who you are, what you want to become, and what you want to achieve.

The stories we have shared with you in this book are not the usual kinds of case studies you read at business school, hear in executive development programs, or will find in your favorite management publication. The leaders who have worked with us and spoken with us for *The Journey of Leadership* did a rare and brave thing. They shared their inner struggles, their doubts, their hopes, their setbacks, and their reinvention stories in the name of helping you to learn how to be a better leader by embracing the principles we've outlined in this book.

We hope that readers of this book will walk away with personal insights that will set them off on a long-term journey to positive change. Yes, it's challenging work, but that doesn't mean it has to be hard. Sometimes it is more about trying less hard and doing less. It is more about deepening awareness of our conditioning (how do my patterns show up in my behaviors and body, what feels at stake in the moment, what mindset am I falling into, and who am I in this moment?). It's about having self-compassion and committing to disciplined practice; it's about improving existing skills and leadership attributes but also adding new ones. Becoming a human-centric leader who truly leads from the inside out is about drawing the right behavioral conclusions and translating them into personal and collective commitments. It is also about creating space for reflection. A moment of deep insight can unlock a profound shift. It is about being present, with yourself and others.

Getting people to be excited, to show initiative, and to follow you on your journey is both a huge challenge and an opportunity. The one thing we know is that you can't achieve that by following yesterday's playbook. As we argued in the beginning of this book, you need to learn to lead from the inside out. Leadership is now all about personal change, about being the change you want to see in the world, and then inspiring others to follow. Our hope is that *The Journey of Leadership* will act as an illuminating beacon on your own journey to becoming your best self.

ACKNOWLEDGMENTS

Though there are four names on the front of this book's jacket, the heroes are the leaders who contributed their time, experience, and wisdom to the stories that fill its pages. Thank you to all our contributors and their teams for their passion, engagement, collaboration, openness, generosity, and care. The opportunity to share your stories and insights of people-centered leadership and interior strength is our inspiration for writing this book.

There have been many invaluable partners in making this book a reality, the first of whom is Brian Dumaine, the former *Fortune* editor, *Bezonomics* author, and our collaborator from day one. Without Brian we would not have been able to bring the stories and inspiration of the leaders in this book to life. Our special thanks to Raju Narisetti, leader of McKinsey's Global Publishing, for his coaching and guidance that has been instrumental in how we think about this book. We were expertly guided by our wonderful agent Lynn Johnston in our early thinking, and a big thank-you to the amazing team at Penguin Random House, especially Adrian Zackheim, Sabrey Manning, and Niki Papadopoulos. And a special thanks to Merry Sun for her early guidance on the manuscript.

ACKNOWLEDGMENTS

We have had numerous sponsors and sparring partners across McKinsey & Company. We thank Johanne Lavoie for her insights, devotion to this project, and pioneering work for over two decades on leading from the inside out. And Faridun Dotiwala has shared wisdom, experience, and research that have refined our thinking. The McKinsey Global Institute team, our People & Organization solutions team, and our colleagues behind OHI (Organizational Health Index) 4.0 have been essential research and thought partners. We want to offer special thanks to Bower Forum CEO participants and our Bower Forum co-faculty colleagues, who are former CEOs, for sharing their insights from their professional and personal lives and their Bower Forum experiences for the benefit of this book. We also thank our partner colleagues, who are too many to mention by name, for opening up their relationships with CEOs, either as Bower Forum participants or as additional interviewees—their trusted counseling relationships offered access and additional insights from these top leaders.

We would never have arrived at this book if it were not for our experiences co-leading the Bower Forum for many of the thirteen years it has existed, and learnings from the five hundred-plus CEOs who have gone through the program. Claudio Feser founded the Bower Forum in late 2011 and, together with André Andonian and Gautam Kumra, later expanded it across the globe. Thank you for your vision and for helping other leaders grow and learn from the inside out. Thank you to the many other partners who were early adopters and helped the Bower Forum grow to its size and scope of impact today. Special thanks to our other McKinsey Bower Forum faculty coaches for their collaboration and thought partnership. We are grateful to various practice leaders in our firm, and especially our colleague Homayoun Hatami, currently overseeing the firm's Integrated Client Capabilities, for his thought partnership along the way. And especially to Santiago Raymond, whose tireless effort has made everything we've done through the Bower Forum possible. There are many other colleagues at McKinsey & Company whose fingerprints are on this book—to Tim Carter, Greg Siviy, Priyank Sood, Julie Wong, Sophia Kummers, and the countless others who have contributed, we are extremely grateful.

Finally, we are collectively grateful for the vision and leadership of Marvin Bower, who led McKinsey & Company to become the firm it is today. This is a home where we have all grown in our own leadership and careers. There have been many incredible leaders who have carried on his legacy at McKinsey, but Ron Daniel, who has been a trusted counselor for us in our own personal journeys, is foremost among them. We also want to express our gratitude to Ian Davis and Dom Barton, our former managing global partners, and our current global managing partner, Bob Sternfels, for supporting the Bower Forum and its own institutional development over all the years.

Each of us has others in our lives who have supported and contributed to this project whom we would also like to thank:

Dana: I joined McKinsey looking to solve the world's toughest problems. As a computer science engineer, I was set on technology and technology strategy. A decade of work taught me that solving the intellectual questions could be hard, but the real hard work was in engaging people and unleashing the power of the organization to act. Attending one of our own leadership programs opened up a new chapter for me. This has become the essence of my personal and professional journey since. I believe that every moment is an opportunity to learn and grow as leaders, and I am fulfilled by this work. I am thankful to my colleagues who trust me with this canvas, my clients who have the courage to engage in this journey with me and McKinsey, my teachers in yoga, leadership, and people, and of course my family, without whom I would not have had the privilege to be on this journey.

Hans-Werner: Early on in my career, I studied leaders in business, politics, history, and other fields of society, and tried to learn especially from those who moved their organizations and people by the combination of heart and mind. Joining McKinsey provided me with the opportunity not only to work with CEOs and other leaders on solutions to their business issues, but to help them in their own leadership journeys and in their efforts to mobilize and inspire their teams and organizations. As such, my passion for human-centric leadership, especially for reinvention journeys, has unfolded and has become the common thread in my professional work. I reinvented myself a few times, from a military career plan to science and then business with leadership journeys at the core. I am grateful to my clients and colleagues, who have been both partnering and learning with me on this journey, and to my coaches and mentors at McKinsey, and especially my family, who have been supporting me in every phase of my journey.

Kurt: Growing up in a family of educators, I've always believed that human capital is as important as all other kinds of capital. Consequently, I want to thank the many people beyond our author group who have created the collective platform of our Bower Forums and our counseling of CEOs globally. One of the most inspiring things about McKinsey is the number of experiments and partnerships in human learning happening with CEOs around the world at any given time. I owe much personally to the CEOs I've been privileged to serve or have helped my colleagues serve. I thank them for the trust, learning mindsets, and ambitions they have brought to our partnerships. Knowing such talented people and their arcs through time as leaders has been an immense part of my own (indirect) leadership journey.

Ramesh: My journey of leadership was triggered by events in my personal life that pushed me to search deeply within for my own purpose. To bring my smile and optimism to the world is what makes me wake up and drives me every day. I am grateful for all the professional help I have received along the way, and for the friends and family who have nurtured me in my journey. I am thankful to my colleagues and clients, who have been incredible teachers and mentors. Last but not least is my wife, Charuta Joshi, who has been an incredible grounding force in my life.

Finally, we thank you, our readers, for your interest in this book. We want to continue to improve ourselves and have greater impact with each successive work, and in this spirit, we welcome any feedback you're willing to share. You can reach us at Leadership_Journey@mckinsey.com.

APPENDIX

MICRO-PRACTICES

In this book we've learned how leaders reinvented themselves, how they became more present, more caring, more aware, more curious, and how through those qualities they raised their effectiveness. What we've discovered is that while the best leaders each have their own style, they consciously apply a set of universal micro-practices that help them keep improving what we call their personal operating model—the way you see yourself and present yourself to others. These could be rituals that you do every day, every week, or every month that help you become who you are at your best. They help you lead with purpose, clarity, and ever-expanding impact.

With this in mind, we compiled one hundred of our favorite micro-practices and categorized them by the three dimensions essential for becoming a great leader: leading yourself, leading individuals and teams, and leading organizations. This list is not exhaustive, and what works for someone else might not work for you. Please pick and choose from our menu of micro-practices to see what best suits your situation, leadership style, and overall way of working.

Leading Self

Leading others first requires the ability to lead yourself by enhancing your self-awareness. It involves deepening your understanding of what fuels your energy, what you value, and what emotions are easy or hard for you to experience. It requires deep introspection and candid self-observation.

1. **Put being before doing.**
   - **Remember your purpose and values.** Write down your top five values and a personal "purpose statement" on a sticky note and put it on your mirror or desk where you will see it regularly.
   - **Cultivate mindfulness.** Whether it's through silence, contemplation, or other meditative practices, have a routine to expand awareness and focus the mind.
   - **Create a "to be" list.** Start each day by writing down one to three attributes you want to embody by asking yourself what people will most need from you and practicing them at work.

2. **Pause for productive reflection and solitude.**
   - **Reflect in the morning.** Go for a walk without your phone and think about the day ahead, your to-do list, and key priorities. If you have a dog, make him or her your accountability buddy!
   - **Reflect after meetings.** Don't jump right into your next task after a big meeting or event, but ask yourself, "What

emotions did I experience? Did I get triggered? If so, what felt at stake and how did I react?"

- **Keep a journal.** Set aside fifteen minutes daily to reflect on your thoughts and actions over the day; consider when you were at your best, and what triggered negative reactions. Focus on one achievable priority for the next day.

3. Seek and embrace feedback from others.

- **Build a core group of truth tellers.** On a regular basis, ask people from both your personal and professional lives what they've observed about your behavior when you're at your best and when you're not. Discuss how your behavior impacts them.
- **Don't wait.** Ask for feedback as quickly as appropriately possible after an event while it is still fresh in people's minds.
- **Look ahead.** Share your growth goals and priorities with others and ask for forward-looking advice.

4. Keep learning.

- **Set goals.** Whether you prefer books, audiobooks, or podcasts, ask others what they are reading or listening to and set targets (for example, three to five books every month).
- **Expand your horizons.** Set aside a long block of time (for example, four hours on the weekend, one Friday afternoon per month) to take a deep dive on priority topics outside your regular areas of expertise.
- **Learn at the source.** Engage directly with those on the front line (analysts, customers, suppliers) rather than reading findings in a report.

- **Connect with experts.** Talk with highly knowledgeable people; there is no faster way to learn than a two-hour walk with a true expert.

5. Embrace optimism.
    - **Cultivate your sense of gratitude.** Start and end each day by reflecting on five things you are grateful for.
    - **Be solutions oriented:** Shift your focus from the problem to solutions by figuring out what is within your control or your influence. Instead of asking "What is the problem?" ask "What do I/we need to solve for?"
    - **Surround yourself with optimists.** Send check-in notes to individuals who consistently uplift and inspire you inside and outside of work.

6. Create new sources of inspiration.
    - **Use great leaders as role models.** Read widely to learn from great leaders through historic novels, biographies, or famous speeches.
    - **Spend quality time with people.** Accept invitations to visit colleagues' homes and cultivate personal friendships when appropriate.
    - **Find a hobby.** Dedicate two hours a week (on a weekday evening or early morning) to what gives you energy and fulfillment outside of work and family.
    - **Seek the space where you have the best ideas.** Ask yourself questions in the shower or while brushing your teeth at night; you may very well wake up with the answer.

7. Be open to those closest to you.
   - **Be transparent.** Share your weekly calendar with your partner or close family and friends.
   - **Share your thoughts.** At the end of each week, share with your partner or a close friend the main themes of your personal reflections and what you wrote in your journal.
   - **Check in.** At the end of each day send a short note or text to someone you care about but have not seen in a while.
   - **Prioritize the big rocks.** Define a few family priorities (for instance, vacations, special events involving the kids, daily or weekly rituals) that you will protect at all costs, treating them with the same or more importance as work.

8. Cultivate physical, mental, spiritual, and emotional health.
   - **Set firm scheduling rules.** Set aside a regular time for important personal priorities (meals, meditation, family, exercise) and do not allow anyone to schedule over them.
   - **Find time-saving ways to shape your holistic fitness habits.** Enlist a trainer, use a fitness app or online food and grocery services.
   - **Be ergonomic.** Take short breaks to stretch, and use a standing desk.
   - **Know yourself.** Enlist a coach or a therapist to check in regularly on your mental health even if you are doing fine.

9. Find ways to refresh yourself.
   - **Practice conscious breathing techniques.** Close your eyes, bring your attention inward, and take a few deep breaths to center and ground yourself. Feel your feet on the ground.

Focus on your breath as you slowly inhale through your nose, hold, and do a longer exhale from your mouth as you relax your body. Repeat until you feel more calm and focused.

- **Set a time to turn off.** If the nature of your job allows it, try to leave the office or shut down your computer at a scheduled time each day. On your way home, call your partner, if you have one, to talk about your workday so that when you arrive you're less preoccupied and more emotionally available.
- **Take sleep seriously.** As often as possible, get at least seven hours of sleep each night and keep your phone in a different room so your most precious time for renewal isn't disturbed.
- **Practice mindfulness.** Take time between meetings or at the start of or end of your day to reset your mind by practicing a quick meditation, prayer, or contemplation.

10. **Find the right balance between personal and professional life.**
    - **Separate work and living spaces.** Have a dedicated room or corner where you work at home. Avoid working in areas associated with relaxation such as the bedroom or living room.
    - **Set technology boundaries.** Have separate phones for work and personal activity. Turn off notifications during mealtimes and when you sleep.
    - **Be clear about boundaries.** Share your boundaries with your assistants and colleagues, including your availability outside normal working hours.

- **Use physical cues.** Mark the transition between work and personal time by changing into work clothes at the beginning of the day and changing back into casual attire at the end of the day.

Leading Individuals and Teams

Leadership is inherently about relationships. Great leaders are human-centric and deliberately invest in improving the way they interact with others. These micro-practices are designed to foster more personal and productive relationships with individuals and teams.

1. **Be attentive.**
   - **Practice active listening.** Ask clarifying questions to ensure you understand not only what someone is saying but also their underlying thoughts, feelings, beliefs, and interests. Put aside your quick judgments and engage meaningfully in conversation, focusing on the other person versus getting your point across.
   - **Cut out distractions and stop multitasking.** During meetings put your phone away, turn off notifications, and don't look at your inbox.
   - **Play it back.** Restate what you've heard from others in your own language and ask for confirmation or clarification to ensure you're accurately capturing what they've shared.
   - **Clear your head.** Before going into a meeting, write down your thoughts so that you aren't distracted by them in the meeting. You'll have a reminder to pick up your train of thought once the meeting is finished.

2. Foster learning and growth.
   - **Become a coach.** Commit to a specific number of people (but not so many that you can't fully commit) with diverse backgrounds whom you want to mentor.
   - **Ask about their goals.** Start one-on-one coaching or feedback sessions by asking about the person's development or professional goals. Write them down and revisit them regularly when you're together.
   - **Bring others with you.** For key interactions with stakeholders, invite one of your mentees along to learn and develop.

3. Give feedback.
   - **Keep track of your feedback.** For each team member, take five minutes after key events to write down your thoughts about and examples of how they performed to bring up in future feedback sessions.
   - **Establish a regular cadence.** Set up time (perhaps biweekly) to provide structured feedback based on the company's established evaluation criteria.
   - **Ask them how you're doing.** During feedback conversations, seek input on how you can better support your people, listen actively, and show appreciation for any positive and constructive feedback you receive.

4. Build confidence and an ownership mindset on your team.
   - **Encourage dissent.** Remind teams at the start of sessions that you value multiple perspectives. Constantly ask, "Where am I wrong?" or "What am I missing?"

- **Engage all voices.** Open decision-making sessions with voices other than your own and allow time for debate. Invite silent voices to speak and coach the dominant ones to create space.
- **Affirm contributions.** Praise people who step up and positively contribute to your team success, and be specific in your praise.

5. Celebrate the big things and the little things.
   - **Encourage colleagues to acknowledge achievements.** Shift conversations away from complaints and encourage others to share their accomplishments so the team can learn from their successes and become more willing to take risks outside their comfort zone. Ask colleagues what they are most proud of in their work.
   - **Reach out.** Spend travel time or other breaks in your calendar to call or email team members to thank them for their contributions or celebrate successes.
   - **Engage others in celebrating wins.** Establish formal celebrations and focus on the learnings. For example, have the management team select an employee of the week; create an annual awards ceremony to celebrate individual achievements that are voted on by the entire organization.

6. Delegate what is not yours to do.
   - **Learn to let go.** Look back at your calendar every Friday and assess which meetings really required your presence based on what only you can do. Identify the meetings outside this boundary and tell your team you trust them to handle them moving forward.

- **Know the strengths of your team members.** Spend time learning the skills and aptitudes of each individual team member and then clearly establish ownership of various aspects of the business that are aligned with those individual strengths. When an issue arises, forward it to the appropriate owner instead of handling it yourself.
- **Streamline communication.** Have your team copy you only on a need-to-know basis. When communications come in from someone not on your team, forward the information to the appropriate team member to handle.

7. **Trust those around you and be trustworthy.**
    - **Demonstrate courageous authenticity.** Be transparent about your intentions and about what you are thinking, feeling, and valuing. Making your thoughts explicit will build trust.
    - **Communicate your trust.** During weekly meetings with your top team, be transparent about your expectations and then tell them that you trust them and are relying on them to make it happen. Provide them space to achieve the job without interference.

8. **Show up.**
    - **Attend company and team events.** Make time to show up to important events, while of course prioritizing and balancing your own workload and personal life.
    - **Don't be late.** Schedule breaks between meetings so that you will not be late. If you are going to be a few minutes late, let your team members know and apologize to them.

9. Model vulnerability.

- **Align your words with your emotions.** Learn to express emotions. You can practice this through creative means such as art or music. Also, learn to emote with expression. Sound inspiring if you are inspired; show concern when appropriate.
- **Be open about your inner life.** Start team meetings by sharing what you are thinking and feeling. What are you excited or concerned about? Invite others to open up as well. The quality of dialogue will improve.
- **Share personal stories.** Tell others about some of your most challenging moments and how they have impacted your leadership, or about times when you have failed and what happened.
- **Admit when you don't know.** It's okay to not have all of the answers. In these situations, don't make up an answer. Be transparent and instead focus on connecting your team with the resources they need to get the answer.

10. Demonstrate selfless leadership.

- **Give away the spotlight.** Rather than doing something yourself, invite one of your team members to give the keynote speech, accept the award, introduce the new program, or send the organization-wide email.
- **Take the tough jobs.** When you know a task is likely to face significant pushback or impede on other priorities, take that on yourself rather than delegating it to someone on your team.

Leading Organizations

Leading an organization requires a related but different skillset of micro-practices than leading individuals and teams—your scope is much wider and your audience can include hundreds or thousands of people. Effectively navigating the complexities of organizational leadership requires a strategic blend of macro-level decision making, cultural influence, and the ability to articulate a compelling vision.

1. **Reinforce values and purpose.**
   - **Ask others.** When meeting with employees, ask them whether they feel that they are working with a sense of purpose and what they value most about being part of the organization.
   - **Reinforce values and purpose across the organization.** Create regular opportunities for your employees to remember and reinforce your company's values and purpose. This could include naming meeting rooms after your values, thanking employees when you see them living by the firm's values and purpose, or setting aside a day every year to reflect on purpose and values.
   - **Celebrate values and purpose throughout the organization.** Connect the daily activities of employees across the organization to the broader mission in your conversations and written communications. In company-wide emails, share stories of people living by the organization's values and purpose or host an annual awards ceremony to celebrate people who best demonstrate those values.

2. Master clear communication.

- **Become a great storyteller.** Use anecdotes to communicate messages, especially when they are about the values or behaviors you want to promote.
- **Get a coach.** Find a communications expert who will review your written and oral communication to help you improve your style.
- **Know your message.** Take five minutes before key meetings or presentations and force yourself to synthesize the point you are trying to make into a single sentence or phrase.
- **Test it with an outsider.** Share your writing or speech with your partner, kids, or a friend before delivering and get feedback on what is not clear. Is it clear enough that someone with no familiarity with the topic can follow along?
- **Start with the "why."** First, clearly and concisely state the purpose or motivation behind a project or initiative so that stakeholders can understand the overarching idea. Then follow up with the "what," and then the "how."

3. Be a role model for the rest of the organization.

- **Be open, be human.** Share your personal development plan, tell stories of your own professional mishaps or hurdles in the past.
- **Show up and respond in moments that matter.** Prioritize events where your presence matters, or where there is an issue that you should address. Being timely is important, especially in challenging or significant times when you may need to offer support, encouragement, or assistance.

- **Set the tone on work boundaries.** Protect everyone's time by limiting calls and emails to work hours. Ask people not to respond to emails when on vacation (unless it's a critical emergency that only they can handle). Whatever the boundaries, make them explicit and encourage others in the organization to follow suit.

4. Build capabilities and promote continual learning.
   - **Ask about learning.** Occasionally pose the question "What did you learn last week/month?" to your team and have them do the same with their reports until it cascades through the organization.
   - **Share your learning agenda.** Be transparent about what you are currently trying to learn and encourage all levels of employees to do so as well.
   - **Embed learning rituals.** Integrate structured learning practices into the daily or regular routines of your organization, such as a one-hour session for learning per week, planned "after action reviews," or cross-office site visits.
   - **Inspire those in transition.** Set up reflection and structured learning programs for colleagues changing roles or receiving promotions. Ask them how they want to be different.

5. Engage stakeholders.
   - **Have a personal advisory board.** Gather a wide variety of advisers, including leadership coaches, senior executives, and mentors, to give you input on engaging different stakeholders.

- **Dedicate travel time.** Review your calendar in advance of trips to make sure 30 to 40 percent of your time on the road is spent with customers, suppliers, investors, and other external stakeholders.
- **Connect with the "why."** When you meet with external stakeholders, ask them what matters to them and connect that with what matters to you and the organization.

6. Champion inclusion.
   - **Reach out.** Meet one new person within your organization each week and show up to listen, empathize, and understand their motivations and the challenges they face with vulnerability and an openness to new ideas.
   - **Encourage diverse perspectives.** During company-wide or divisional meetings, proactively seek input from employees with different backgrounds, experiences, and expertise, particularly those from minority backgrounds. Limit the airtime of those who speak often. Ask quieter individuals for their input and listen deeply.
   - **Lead by example.** At events, demonstrate inclusive behavior by welcoming people who are trying to join a conversation. Introduce yourself to a variety of people with a handshake and ask them questions. Show respect, openness, and fairness to set the tone for others.
   - **Define and set goals for inclusion.** Hold people accountable for what inclusion means for your organization. Set conscious business goals to cater to a broader customer or stakeholder base.

7. Adopt a "servant leader" mentality.

   - **Put others first.** Have all the leaders in your organization ask their employees what they can do to make their jobs easier.
   - **Remove obstacles.** When someone says they're facing a hurdle, train your leaders to find ways on the spot to remove it. That could be connecting the person with the appropriate resources or suggesting a few people who can assist.
   - **Demonstrate a willingness to do any task.** Spend a day "on the line," and hold the door for others. If you have employees who take public transit, ride with them one day.

8. Cultivate a growth mindset.

   - **Encourage innovation.** Create a work environment that fosters creativity and experimentation. Celebrate innovative ideas in company-wide emails, hold innovation competitions to develop new ideas around priority topics.
   - **Embrace technological changes.** Receive weekly technology updates on digital trends that may impact your business. Be quick to consult experts and adapt your strategy if necessary, and share findings with key players in your organization.
   - **Learn from failure.** Communicate and celebrate instances where someone learned from a failure to encourage a more agile and risk-taking culture.

9. Incorporate fun in the organization.

   - **Establish time to connect.** Encourage teams across all levels of the organization to schedule time to have fun. It could be a gathering at a local bowling alley, an annual internal Olympics, or a departmental trivia contest.

- **Encourage humor.** Use humor not to avoid the hard messages but to help people open up and take themselves less seriously. Laugh at yourself when you make mistakes; cultivate organization-wide inside jokes and pop culture references in recurring meetings. Find someone who enjoys quick, playful photo editing.

- **Embrace playfulness.** Start large group sessions with a game, hand out prizes, get people up and moving as much as possible.

- **Surprise people.** Plan occasional surprise activities such as ordering in meals or escapes from the office to celebrate, relieve stress, and build camaraderie.

10. **Be decisive, not impulsive.**

- **Ask for advice.** Get input from at least three but no more than five trusted advisers when making a big decision; your advisers should be from both within and outside your organization.

- **Collect broad input.** Seek widespread input from colleagues across various functions, levels, and areas of expertise before making any significant changes to the organization. You can do this via surveys, focus groups, and special task forces. Ensure the input is carefully considered and not simply a rubber stamp.

- **Sleep on it.** When announcing any major decisions, draft the email or memo but wait twenty-four hours before sending it and reflect on your reaction and emotions before hitting send.

BOWER FORUM LEADERSHIP SURVEY AND KEY RESULTS

We conducted a survey of participants from 2018 to 2023 to understand their leadership challenges and what they learned at the Bower Forum. Here is what they told us.

The largest set of challenges that leaders brought into the Bower Forum were personal.

What was the nature of the leadership challenge you put on the table when you participated in the Bower Forum?

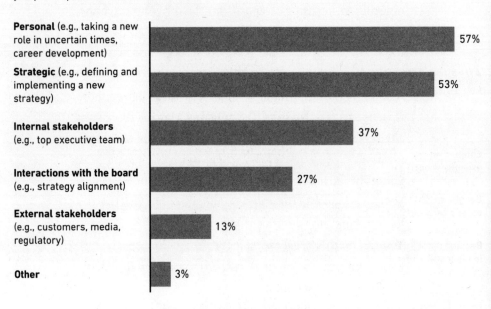

Personal (e.g., taking a new role in uncertain times, career development) — 57%

Strategic (e.g., defining and implementing a new strategy) — 53%

Internal stakeholders (e.g., top executive team) — 37%

Interactions with the board (e.g., strategy alignment) — 27%

External stakeholders (e.g., customers, media, regulatory) — 13%

Other — 3%

The biggest takeaways from the Bower Forum were a broader vision of what is possible and a sense that leaders were not alone in their challenges.

What most shifted in your perspective or mindset as a leader from the Bower Forum or other similar experiences? (Top 5)

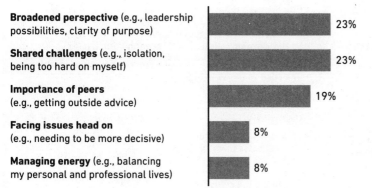

Broadened perspective (e.g., leadership possibilities, clarity of purpose) — 23%

Shared challenges (e.g., isolation, being too hard on myself) — 23%

Importance of peers (e.g., getting outside advice) — 19%

Facing issues head on (e.g., needing to be more decisive) — 8%

Managing energy (e.g., balancing my personal and professional lives) — 8%

After the Bower Forum, many participants have started to work with peers to keep learning and improving their leadership practices.

What new or continued actions did you prioritize coming out of the Bower Forum? (Top 6)

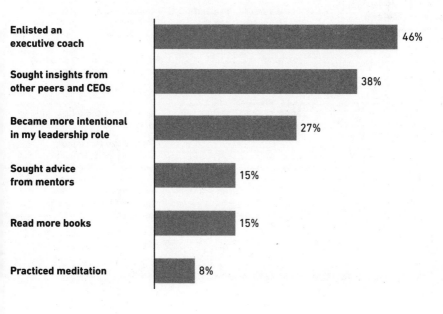

Enlisted an executive coach — 46%

Sought insights from other peers and CEOs — 38%

Became more intentional in my leadership role — 27%

Sought advice from mentors — 15%

Read more books — 15%

Practiced meditation — 8%

HOW MCKINSEY'S BOWER FORUM CEO LEADERSHIP DEVELOPMENT PROGRAM WORKS: OVERVIEW

Assessment—CEOs analyze their situation by discussing their:	*Deep reflection—they then engage in self-assessment followed by the first steps of a reinvention process:*	*They leave with a commitment plan for continual reinvention that includes:*

• Industry and company
• Ecosystem
• Board and management team
• Stakeholders
• Journey as a CEO and as an individual
  ◦ Do they have a clear mandate from the board and other stakeholders?
  ◦ What is their current personal state vs. their desired state?
  ◦ What are the priorities and challenges?
• Main agenda priorities, the related core elements of their mandate, and their leadership practices (self, team, broader organization) that they want to address and improve in the Forum
• Improved self-awareness based on their own feedback and that from others
	CEOs express their aspirations for themselves, their team, and their organization and discuss:
	• The positive forces vs. the barriers
	• Beliefs and assumptions vs. the reality
	• What gives them energy and motivates them vs. what holds them back
	
	CEOs begin the reinvention process:
	• Peer CEOs and faculty members reflect upon the leader's aspirations, positive forces, and counterforces (for individual CEOs and their ecosystem) and engage in peer learning
	• In trust-based "give and take" conversations the group offers advice for moving forward and peer learning
	• CEOs absorb advice during the "deep dive" and provide their reflections and appreciation after the deep dive and peer learning
		A commitment plan for leading themselves, their team, and their organization by:
		• Embedding human-centric leadership attributes in themselves and their organizations
		• Creating a personal "to be" profile that includes self-awareness, vulnerability, and empathy, and then instilling those qualities throughout the organization
		• Mastering the five balancing acts, i.e., being "humble and assertive/bold" and then sharing them with others
		• Working on being a more versatile leader by engaging in deep learning and broadening their experiences
		• Developing a plan with milestones and "check-in" processes
		
		A road map for the ongoing journey of reinvention:
		• Bower Forum faculty and peer CEOs serve as counselors and follow up periodically
		• Respective McKinsey partners write a memo summarizing the Bower Forum experience and learnings and augment the commitment plan for the CEO
		• CEOs, as needed, consult confidants/coaches

Leadership Development Approach and Experience: Learning to Lead from the Inside Out

NOTES

Introduction

xii **It's little wonder:** Development Dimensions International, "Leaders in Transition: Progressing along a Precarious Path," 2015, https://www.ddiworld.com/research/leaders-in-transition-progressing-along-a-precarious-path.

xiii **According to the executive compensation firm:** Joyce Chen, "CEO Tenure Rates," Harvard Law School Forum on Corporate Governance, https://corpgov.law.harvard.edu/2023/08/04/ceo-tenure-rates-2/.

xiii **A survey conducted:** Rasmus Hougaard, Jacqueline Carter, and Rob Stembridge, "The Best Leaders Can't Be Replaced by AI," *Harvard Business Review*, January 12, 2024.

xiv **According to a 2023 McKinsey:** Anu Madgavkar, Bill Schaninger, Dana Maor, Olivia White, Sven Smit, Hamid Samandari, Jonathan Woetzel, Davis Carlin, and Kanmani Chockalingam, "Performance Through People: Transforming Human Capital into Competitive Advantage," McKinsey Global Institute, February 2023, https://www.mckinsey.com/mgi/our-research/performance-through-people-transforming-human-capital-into-competitive-advantage.

xiv **In fact, when the COVID-19:** Madgavkar et al., "Performance Through People."

Part 1: It Starts with You

5 **As a *New Yorker* cartoon:** Roy Delgado, *New Yorker*, October 5, 2007.

5 **As former Warren Buffett sidekick:** Peter D. Kaufman, *Poor Charlie's Almanack: The Essential Wit and Wisdom of Charles T. Munger* (South San Francisco, CA: Stripe Press, 2005).

NOTES

6 **A fierce winter:** "The Retreat from Moscow," britannica.com, https://www.bri
tannica.com/event/Napoleonic-Wars/The-retreat-from-Moscow.

6 **In the 1970s:** Chuck Tannert, "John DeLorean Reinvented the Dream Car. Then
He Totaled It," *Forbes*, July 26, 2019, https://www.forbes.com/wheels/news/john
-delorean-reinvented-the-dream-car-then-he-totaled-it.

20 **She recalls watching:** Brian Draper, "Positive Energy," High Profiles, February
11, 2011, https://highprofiles.info/interview/ellen-macarthur.

34 **In her book *Team of Rivals*:** Doris Kearns Goodwin, *Team of Rivals: The Political
Genius of Abraham Lincoln* (New York: Simon & Schuster, 2006).

62 **Early in his career, Walt Disney:** Patricia Sellers, "So You Fail. Now Bounce
Back!," *Fortune*, May 1, 1995.

65 **Under her guidance:** William B. Barrett, "Food Bank Network Ousts United Way
as America's Largest Charity," *Forbes*, December 13, 2022, https://www.forbes
.com/sites/williampbarrett/2022/12/13/food-bank-network-ousts-united
-way-as-americas-largest-charity/?sh=1f49bc655b1d.

82 **The Center for Automotive Research:** Sam Abuelsamid, "Auto Industry Crisis
Leads to Job Losses Even at Strong Companies," Autoblog, December 20, 2008,
https://www.autoblog.com/2008/12/20/auto-industry-crisis-leads-to-job
-losses-even-at-strong-companie.

84 **He never knew:** Walter Isaacson, *Leonardo da Vinci* (New York: Simon & Schuster,
2017).

86 **At Amazon, Jeff Bezos:** Brian Dumaine, *Bezonomics: How Amazon Is Changing Our
Lives and What the World's Best Companies Are Learning from It* (New York: Scribner,
2020).

89 ***The Wall Street Journal* declared:** Dawn Gilbertson, Allison Pohle, and Kevin
McAllister, "The Best and Worst Airlines of 2023," *Wall Street Journal*, January 24,
2024.

90 **Those who are tempted:** Tim Bontemps, "Michael Jordan Stands Firm on 'Republicans Buy Sneakers, Too' Quote, Says It Was Made in Jest," ESPN, May 4, 2020.

Part 2: Moving beyond Yourself

126 **As Winston Churchill:** Gerben A. van Kleef, *The Interpersonal Dynamics of Emotion*, published online by Cambridge University Press, April 5, 2016, https://www
.cambridge.org/core/books/abs/interpersonal-dynamics-of-emotion/social
-effects-of-emotions-in-leadership/D40CAA59355BE6384796D286881F1625.

126 **A classic example:** Dawn Chmielewski, "No More Red Envelopes: Netflix to
End DVD-by-Mail Business," Reuters, April 18, 2023, https://www.reuters.com
/technology/netflix-winds-down-dvd-rental-business-2023-04-18.

NOTES

131 **In a blog post:** Judy Savitskaya and Jorge Conde, "What Is a Bio Platform For?," Andreessen Horowitz, January 8, 2021, https://a16z.com/what-is-a-bio-platform-for.

146 **After the matchup:** Dave Zangaro, "Hurts' Inspiring Message After Losing the Super Bowl," NBC Sports Philadelphia,

161 **In 1961, President John F. Kennedy:** Stephen Bates and Joshua L. Rosenbloom, "Kennedy and the Bay of Pigs," Kennedy School of Government Case Program, 1998.

163 **McKinsey's research:** Ben Fletcher, Chris Hartley, Rupe Hoskin, and Dana Maor, "Into All Problem-Solving, a Little Dissent Must Fall," McKinsey & Company, February 2023.

178 **The twentieth-century economist:** Keynes is widely cited as the source of this quote, although historians cannot document it.

184 **At Amazon, for example:** Brian Dumaine, *Bezonomics: How Amazon Is Changing Our Lives and What the World's Best Companies Are Learning from It* (New York: Scribner, 2020).

190 **McKinsey's 2023 report:** Anu Madgavkar, Bill Schaninger, Dana Maor, Olivia White, Sven Smit, Hamid Samandari, Jonathan Woetzel, Davis Carlin, and Kanmani Chockalingam, "Performance Through People: Transforming Human Capital into Competitive Advantage," McKinsey Global Institute, February 2023, https://www.mckinsey.com/mgi/our-research/performance-through-people-transforming-human-capital-into-competitive-advantage.

191 **The high-performing companies:** Madgavkar et al., "Performance Through People."

191 **According to the research firm:** Great Place to Work website, July 2019, https://www.greatplacetowork.com/certified-company/1000745.

192 **The survey found:** McKinsey Organizational Health Index team, 2023.

192 **Sadly, three-quarters of respondents:** Mary Abbajay, "What to Do When You Have a Bad Boss," *Harvard Business Review*, September 2018.

202 **A Gallup poll released:** 18 Employee Recognition Statistics You Need to Know, *Workhuman*, September 2023, https://www.workhuman.com/blog/employee-recognition-statistics/.

INDEX

INDEX

Chapman, Bob, 189–90, 193–202
charity, 201
Chase, Salmon P., 34
Chatham Rules, xv
chess, 182
China, 137–38, 165
Chouinard, Yvon, 108–9
Chrysler, xi, 82
Churchill, Winston, 126
CIA, 179
Ciba-Geigy, 11–12
Cincinnati Children's Hospital Medical
 Center, 27–28, 58, 81, 95, 96
Cincinnati USA Regional Chamber of
 Commerce, 81
Citibank, 69–71
Citicorp, 24
Citigroup, 13
Civil War, 34
climate change, 90, 93–95, 103, 108, 111, 119
Clinton, Bill, 154
Clinton Global Initiative, 154
Coca-Cola, 63
Cognizant, 120–21, 149–53, 205–6
Collins, Jim, 151
commitment plan, 209, 214–20
 advisers and, 220
 behaviors and changes in, 214–15
 example of, 218–19
 reviewing of, 216, 220
 three basic elements of, 217–18
 tools in, 215–16
communication, clarity in, 241
compassion and empathy, 51, 122, 174,
 189–209
Conde, Jorge, 131
confidence, 19–31, 33, 34, 37, 44,
 78, 125, 129
Constitution, U.S., 195

contributory dissent, 163–64
control, as illusion, 145–59
Costco, 191
courage, 18, 31, 73, 87, 206, 212, 238
 boldness, 124, 125–44, 150, 181, 210, 213
COVID-19 pandemic, xiv, 53, 81,
 88–89, 96, 116–18, 128–29, 135,
 136, 145, 203
 vaccines and, 96, 127–34
Crack-Up, The (Fitzgerald), xix
credibility, 33
CreditEase, 70
criticism, 10, 57, 172
Cuba, 161–62
cultural literacy, 25–27, 54
culture, workplace, 36–39, 112, 139–42, 205
 dignity in, 195, 197, 201
 fear-based, 149
 "heroes, rituals, and legends" model
 for, 205–6
 male-dominated, 21–22, 24
 management of, 175
 openness in, 162
 secrecy in, 166–67
 strategy and, 175
curiosity, 73, 78, 79, 84–86, 129, 170, 171,
 184, 210, 212
customer satisfaction, 152, 206

data, 40, 54
Davos, World Economic Forum in, 70,
 71, 128–30
Deci, Edward, 151
decision making, 13, 14, 18, 29, 31, 33, 34,
 37, 39–41, 44, 56–58, 117, 125, 151,
 159, 169, 171, 186, 212
 Big Four system for, 183–84
 boldness in, 124, 125–44, 150, 181,
 210, 213

INDEX

INDEX